STRATEGIC
THINKING
and
INSIGHTS

STRATEGIC
THINKING
and
INSIGHTS

Teck Choon TEO & Kim Cheng Patrick LOW

PARTRIDGE

To order additional copies of this book, contact
Toll Free 800 101 2657 (Singapore)
Toll Free 1 800 81 7340 (Malaysia)
orders.singapore@partridgepublishing.com

www.partridgepublishing.com/singapore

CONTENTS

Foreword

After reading this book, do not be surprised to find yourself becoming conscious of strategies and strategic leadership and managing of people. And/or better still, be very much aware of strategic and meaningful living! And work well but work smartly and strategically.

Teo and Low's Strategic Thinking and Insights is what strategies are all about. The basic premise of this book is to develop and grow good strategies when it comes to business, management and leadership– since it could be a war or a jungle out there! Of course, we always want to better our strategies to improve our businesses; otherwise, our businesses will suffer.

To stress, it is not just a book on Singapore Company and strategic thinking and insights, but rather one that is rightly relevant to anyone in any country. The future and our destiny is really in our own hands; it's up to us. We are what we want to be. And undeniably so, for us to flourish; we must emulate excellence to become excellent.

Teo and Low's Strategic Thinking and Insights can indeed serve as a guide – and checklists can be derived from it; one can also read the book from time to time to pick strategic thinking tips and ideas.

Certainly so, many strategic pointers exist in this book that will hasten and encourage you on! I wish you well; and that you reap the harvest from this book! May you be inspired and have the will power to attain your goals! And more importantly, you act on the strategies learnt! After all, strategy(ies) without action is useless, and a strategy(ies) without action is no strategy at all.

Happy reading!

Dr. Alpamys T. Ibrayev
President of Kazakhstan's Academy of Information and Business,
Doctor of Mathematical and Physical Science

Foreword

"Think any way you please, but know why."

Martin H. Fischer (1879–1962)

Strategic thinking is defined as a mental, psychological or thinking process applied by a person in the setting of attaining victory in a game or other endeavour. As a cognitive activity, it produces thought. When applied in an organisational strategic management process, strategic thinking involves the generation and application of unique business insights and opportunities intended to create competitive edge for a company or an organisation.

Why goal-setting is so critical? Discussing strategies and knowing why are the heart of Teo and Low's Strategic Thinking and Insights. This book seeks to develop and nurture reliable or helpful strategies when it comes to business, people management and in leadership – since it could be a war or a jungle out there! It is always beneficial and useful to find and develop a strategic foresight capacity for one's organisation, by exploring all possible organisational futures, and challenging conventional thinking to foster decision making today. Hence, this is a book recommended for one to ignite or gather helpful thoughts for eventual use and/ or applications.

After perusing through this book, do not be surprised to find yourself becoming more aware of strategies and strategic direction and management of people. And/or better still, be very much aware of strategic and meaningful living! And do well but do smartly and strategically.

A good strategist must ordinarily have a great gift for both analysis (seeing the individual tree(s) and synthesis (seeing the forest as a whole). Analysis or examination is necessary to assemble the data on which (s)he makes his(her) diagnosis, synthesis in order to produce from these data the diagnosis itself—and the diagnosis in fact totals to an option between alternative courses of action. And here, Teo and Low's Strategic Thinking and Insights can certainly serve as a suitable guide – with checklists or worksheets gained from it; one can also read the book from time to time to pick advantageous, if not cutting edge, strategic thinking and/or formulating ideas.

Positively so, many strategic tips exist in this book that will hasten and incite you on! I sincerely wish you well; and that you reap the generous harvest from this book! May you be enthused and stirred and have the resolve to accomplish your goals!

Happy reading!

HUA Pak Cheong
BSc (Econ) (London), MBA (Strathclyde)
Accredited Practising Management Consultant (Singapore Business Advisors & Consultants Council)

Preface

Globalisation and global marketplace is today's reality. A truly global marketplace is fast emerging. Competition is fast and furious; the intense competition has forced many companies in nearly every country to be leaner, perhaps meaner and more flexible: to meet their customers' demands and more importantly, to seek out new opportunities. We need to develop strategic, creative and/ or innovative ways for our organisations and ourselves to succeed. Give it a twist, massage, adapt and give it a GO! And to paraphrase the then Singapore's Prime Minister, Mr. Goh Chok Tong – If the ice *kacang* man can do it, you can do too! (The Straits Times, 5 Apr 2000, p. 1).

It is not just a book on Singapore companies and strategic thinking and insights, but rather one that is applicable to anyone anywhere in any country. The future is really in your hands; it is up to you! And indeed, individuals must succeed, getting ahead; and companies must become or emulate to be excellent organisations.

This book tells you:

What is adversarial thinking?

What is strategic thinking?

How do you set personal goals?

Why is goal-setting so critical?

When presenting, what guidelines or a framework can we resort to for on-the-spot thinking?

Looking at a particular topic from various angles or different perspectives.

What is preventive thinking?

The what-to-dos, and ways of getting ahead in one's career.

What is forward thinking & planning?

The benefits of planning.

What is organisational goal-setting?

The whys and wherefores of organisational goal-setting.

What and how to achieve organisational effectiveness?

Recreating the company – Ways to avoid 'groupthink'.

What are competitive and co-operative strategies?

What create successful business alliances?

What are the criteria in building successful inter-organisational relationships?

Designing organisations and the benefits of self-directing teams.

What are the major traits of excellent and successful organisations?

And a dozen of other things you should know about strategic thinking. Essentially, there are listed in this book various techniques and strategies for enhancing your career, if not making you differentiated or stand out!

Read on! You will enjoy reading this reader-friendly book, as much as I do in putting the ideas together. You could also get various tips and pointers on thinking on your feet during presentations, planning and thinking strategically for both your career progress and your company's successes. And what's more, my dear friends; I challenge you to look forward to seize opportunities that await proactive people in this new century. No one else can succeed for you!

Teck Choon TEO and Kim Cheng Patrick LOW

Chapter 1

Introduction

"If foresight is not the whole of management, at least, it is an essential part of it."

Henri Fayol

At the launch of the 7th International Conference on Thinking in June 1997, the then Singapore's Prime Minister Mr Goh Chok Tong highlighted that "we will bring a mindset change among Singaporeans. We must get away from the idea that it is only the people at the top who should be thinking and the job of everyone else is to do as told. Instead, we want to bring a spirit of innovation, of learning by doing, of everyone each at his own level all the time asking how he can do his job (***and thinking***) better" (*italics added*, mine).

Have you been doing your job well? Can it be better performed? Or are you taking your job for granted? Have you been thinking, finding ways to do your job better? Are there ways to do your job better? Are there ways to do your job thinking better? Are you a thinker? What sort of thinker are you? Are you a strategic thinker?

Strategic Thinking

But what is strategic thinking?

Strategic thinking is the ultimate test of a leader. It is the move from being clever to being wise. Strategic thinking is about making long-term decisions and direction. It is also about making a difference.

Strategic thinking is the ability to see things at different angles, covering a number of grounds and perspectives. It must be expansive thinking, looking at the various possibilities with the aim to better oneself or the organisation as well as achieve positions of sustained advantage with higher, and more secured returns.

At the individual level, when we do strategic thinking, we are actually self-empowering ourselves – thinking about our personal marketing, self-renewal plus the skills needed to reach our goals. Nowadays, so many things can happen, uncertainty is certain and new trends are emerging. And how in sync are you with the emerging trends? What do you see as beneficial? Are you capitalising on any of these trends?

New players, getting-better-qualified entrants will always come to the job market. Supply of a highly educated work force exists; its supply is greater than demand that frequently leads to underemployment. Improved IT and tele-communications are also accommodating the use of low-cost technical talent, abroad in decentralised business operational units. Also, with technological innovations and globalisation, restructuring, downsizing, and outsourcing are taking place to streamline business operations, enabling them to be more competitive. Companies should be more socially responsible, as resources too are getting more limited. In fact, the resources are more life-threateningly polluted than they used to be. Companies have to be greener while doing more with less. They are getting more results with less, eliminating many staff and middle management positions. And added to these, temporary workers are nowadays increasingly being used. A diverse service and small business economy is also fast appearing to be quite common and much opportunity exists too. And what are we doing about it? Should we not be thinking strategically too? From what's happening out there, are we opening up new horizons and possibilities for ourselves?

Strategic thinking will be your best friend when you find yourself needing or wanting to make a move. It is a mind-growth that is geared to the benefits of new events, it is a resolve to think and do whatever may be required to achieve a better you. You can move ahead of your life.

Strategic thinking is, in our view, as mentioned by Confucius in the Lun Yu (The Analects) that we are to "emulate the strength of others and use their weaknesses for self-correction".

Setting Goals

To think strategically is to set goals, giving us stars to steer by. We drift like a jellyfish along with tide when we do not set or have no goals for ourselves. You need to have a pocket or a bag to hold something. Goals serve as pockets or bags to fill things or more specifically, hold our achievements. Goals are energising; goals set us to achieve. They give us the necessary high drive and physical energy. They enable us to stay on course!

What are the secrets of high achievers? One of the secrets of these successful people is that they have goals. Nothing is ever gained if one doesn't set a goal to achieve what one wants. When there are no goals, there are no results. In academic life for example, I believe that there is no such thing as a lazy student but rather one who does not set a goal or goals!

Goals DIRECT OUR LIVES. You must design goals that will consciously drive and direct you to great success!

When you set goals you are telling your inner self, what you want and work towards achieving them. People who rarely or do not set goals rarely achieve what they want in life. The first step to success is the goal that you set for yourself.

Ask yourself what you want in life. What are the various wants? What do you want? Where are you now? Where are you heading? Where are you going?

First of all, write your dream. Write your goal! You are setting the stage to know what you want. You cannot see it, you are not reminded of it! You cannot see it, you cannot hit it! Just as in a dart game, you must see the target to hit it. And avoid distractions; take whatever obstacles as the frightful things you see when you take your mind off your goals.

Indeed Dr. Judy Lim, a successful lady corporate leader advises on the need to be clear about our goals. "If you are not clear on what you want, you cannot begin to find what you wish to achieve." And in fact, she goes on to say that this clarity vision must be matched by a commitment to see the goal through (The Straits Times, 12 January 1998).

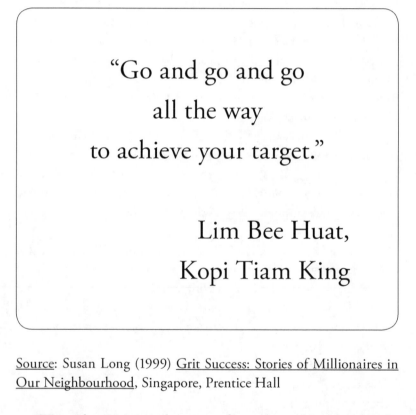

"Go and go and go
all the way
to achieve your target."

Lim Bee Huat,
Kopi Tiam King

Source: Susan Long (1999) Grit Success: Stories of Millionaires in Our Neighbourhood, Singapore, Prentice Hall

We can have many goals, ranging from relationships/ social goals, family, spiritual /peace of mind to health, and wealth (prosperity), and also to academic goals or to something hopeful and related to the future or long-term goals.

How is it felt, what did you feel when arranging or organising for a great birthday party, a vacation, an overseas trip, or going to a place where you have not been before? Get your goals to be big and exciting and you would have had geared up or psyched yourself to achieve them.

We indeed need to set **S.M.A.R.T**. goals.

Our goals need to be **S**pecific. Before you shoot an arrow, you must have a target. You need to know your definite destination before you start on your journey!

Goals must also be **M**easurable – it must be done step-by step and can be counted or quantifiable.

And if for example, you are now studying – as a student, finding ways and means, praying, wanting and getting the marker to be more lenient or be less strict when marking your exam scripts is unrealistic. What grade(s) do you want to attain and what steps are you taking to attain such grade(s)? Goals should be **A**ttainable & **R**ealistic. These goals must be able attainable yet challenging. Tan Jin Heng, Managing Director of HTE Engineering advises aspiring entrepreneurs, "Stay focused… Have clear objectives (goals) and try to set targets that are realistic and achievable" (Khoo, Catherine and Chua Chong Jin; 2000: 75).

Goals need to be **T**ime-based too. Goals need to be time-bound. Without time-based goals, we tend to procrastinate. We defer things; "leave it to tomorrow" and tomorrow never comes. Indeed, we need to be aware of the "tomorrow syndrome". Being time-based helps, it gives us an action plan with a deadline. There's no point talking but without action, it becomes NATO: No Action, Talk Only! A schedule or a timetable must be worked out.

Additionally, we build some S T R E T C H into our goals – otherwise we under-achieve. True, goal(s) must be S.M.A.R.T. And while one stretches oneself, one, however, needs to have faith and trust in oneself in achieving the goals. Be true to yourself! Belief in yourself!

We need to believe in goals. Our beliefs will influence our attitude and goals. Beliefs are like mountains. Some mountains are higher than other mountains. Some mountains are tall; some are lower. Some beliefs are strong while some are weak. Weak beliefs are negative values; they are unhealthy or damaging to wholesome living. Weak values result in loss of a loved one, problems at work, inability to secure employment, etc.

Strong beliefs are positive values, one that helps us in our living. Positive beliefs are empowering. It reinforces good habits. Beliefs in determination and independence help us to survive as a nation, the will to live and sustain ourselves. Such beliefs make Singaporeans resilience. Belief in adversity helps us. The *"pukul tak mati!"* belief or being tough and determined (*"uruthi"* – Tamil word) is also great – it builds us, makes us turn adversities into advancements, problems into opportunities. Next, the belief in technology helps us to make progress. Such belief leads us to tap the power of technology and be forward-looking. Also, another powerful positive belief is that of believing in yourself!

Here's something for you!

Reflect! Do identify and reinforce any beliefs you have that will move you in the directions of your goals. (Remember positive beliefs have the Pygmalion Effect; they have the power of expectations and enhance your performance.)

As you do this, it's also time for you to get rid of beliefs, particularly negative, dis-empowering beliefs that no longer serve you! Kill these negative beliefs, the monsters while they are little!

Believe in yourself!

One can only rely on oneself; and remember nobody owes anyone a living.

What you achieve or fail to achieve in life, is directly related to what you do or what you fail to do. To the authors, there is no failures but what one can learn in life and apply to our lives to improve our position and overall lives.

No one chooses his parents or his childhood, but you can choose your own vision and direction. You can choose your own strategy (direction).

Everyone has problems and obstacles to overcome, but that too, is relative to each individual.

Nothing is carved in stone or cast in iron, you can change anything in your life, if you want to do well enough.

Excuses are for losers; those who take responsibility for their actions are the real winners in life.

Winners meet challenges head on, knowing that there are no guarantees; yet winners give it all they've got.

And never think it's too late or early to begin, time plays no favourites and will pass whether you act or not.

Take charge; take control of your life.

Dare to dream, take risks and compete.

If you are not willing to work for your goals, don't expect others to.

Believe in yourself!

We need to state our goals in the positive way, better when we do so in the present continuous tense. This suggests that the goals are being realised. For example, as a student, it is better to write – "I am committed to doing well, I'm getting an 'A' for history" as my goal than "I will be scoring an A for my history". When you write it in the future, your subconscious mind will take it as a future and it has found to work in such a way that the future will always remain in the future. So, remember, state your goals as if they are happening now!

Indeed, as corporate leaders and managers, like it or not, we have to be strategic thinkers – people who can contribute and be more productive! If we are going to be successful, we need to be creative, pro-active, action-driven – "do it!" and be effective at getting things done.

Adversarial Thinking versus Strategic Thinking

Broadly speaking, two categories of people exist; one is the adversarial thinker who is rather passive, even negative and at times, avoids action or getting things done. The other is the strategic thinker who is pro-active person and creatively gets things done.

The adversarial thinker can be hindered, restricted or immobilised by any weakness(es), theirs or their people. At times, they concentrate too much in trying to overcome or right these weaknesses. The strategic thinker, however, plays to his or her strengths. (S)he also heeds to emulating the strengths of others. And (s)he capitalises on any or all of these strengths and in strength (s)he grows.

While adversarial thinkers resist change and seek stability or security, strategic thinkers wholeheartedly embrace and in fact, are committed to adding value. Strategic thinkers would prod on, searching for better alternatives.

Since they adopt a 'get' attitude – always wanting to receive – adversarial thinkers are hesitant to support new ideas for fear of losing power or incurring risks. They may not be entrepreneurial, afraid of taking risks. Sticking to the old ways and hesitate to support new ideas, they inadvertently repeat past mistakes. Strategic thinkers, on the other hand, take a 'give' view of life, willing to take risks and innovate. Indeed, they encourage innovations, creating new alternatives and options for their company, people and themselves.

With a security orientation and image consciousness, adversarial thinkers tend to work towards maintaining the status quo or working towards avoiding mistakes. The adversarial thinker would also seek refuge in his or her position, up-keeping power. (S)he may hide behind policies, procedures and the company's set (bureaucratic) ways. On the other hand, emphasising more on (long-term) results and growth, strategic thinkers would change ineffective policies and procedures. And thriving well in a changing (often, interpreting it as a challenging) environment, strategic thinkers work to achieve. They rise to the occasion. More eager to initiate or lead, the strategic thinkers also use the company's structure to support progress. They build their contacts or relationships, create teams, strengthen ties and partnerships to achieve, and together they achieve even more.

In terms of motivation, adversarial thinkers are more motivated by fear, the fear of loss of their positions and power. Strategic thinkers, on the other hand, are more motivated by a sense of purpose. They feel more like they are the masters of their destiny. They seek to marshal their circumstances. Indeed, they usually ask themselves, "At this point, what am I capable of, even more so than before?"

In short, the adversarial thinkers are more prone to postponing with the tendency to institutionalise the past while the strategic thinkers look forward and create the future.

Your Notes, Ideas
& Action Points

Chapter 2

Thinking On Your Feet

*"Hi! Mate, would do me a favour? Please do lend
1,000 yen?"*
"Yes, why not?"
"Thank you"
*"Oh, no prob (problem)! But I also have a favour to ask
of you."*
"Anything you say, I'll do!"
*"Mmm... you see I find it difficult to say but, say,
could you take back the request you've just made."*
                                                    A Japanese Story

*Two explorers were moving rather slowly across the icy
wastes*
*when suddenly, a polar bear reared up from behind a
glacier.*
"What do we do now?" cried one of the men.
*The other man knelt down, removed his snowshoes and
took a pair of trainers out of his knapsack.*
*"It's no point putting those on, those bears can outrun any
man", said the first man.*
*"I know", replied the other, "but I only have to run faster
than you."*

To be a strategic thinker, all of us must also think on our feet.
When we talk or communicate with others, we will talk and present
ourselves well when we think on our feet. We need to practise

thinking on our feet. Thinking on our feet means thinking quickly, presenting ideas and on the spot, coming up with plausible answers. It is only through practise that we can really prefect, if not better such skills. Practise, practise, practise! Remember that raindrops can even wear down stone.

But how can we practise thinking on the feet, thinking fast and plausibly? How can we analyse, organise and present our ideas persuasively or variedly? What are the techniques involved?

Let us explain.

Using Both Sides of Our Brain, Are We Doing It?

When we want to start thinking on our feet, first of all we exploit both sides of our brain, the left and the right hemispheres of our forebrain. The left side is usually used for logical thinking, sequential and step-by-step. On the other hand, the right hemisphere is responsible for our intuition, imagination and emotions. The right side of our forebrain also enables us to see the big picture, the synthesis. We need to use or connect both sides of our brain to better our thinking.

To think on our feet and speak confidently without notes, we need to connect our left brain to the right brain. We need to plan and planning a left brain function. We need to think about our listeners' viewpoints and issues vital to their interests. We also need to deliver and delivering a speech without notes is a right brain function. Do use our emotions, feel our expressions and express our feelings. At the same, do focus on our audience's feelings too. Yes, do grip the audience. Ask ourselves: what are their hopes and fears?

Planning – Thinking Ahead

Have plans, three-part plans, structure your speech: introduction, body and conclusion or ending. Remember the first and the last impressions always register strongly.

On one hand, introductions should raise the audience's interest and curiosity. And the endings should, on the other hand, recap or summarises your talk. The ending should also jolt people to action or at least they end up knowing what to do next.

Delivering

Strategise your presentation.

In terms of delivery, I would simply use a mind map or idea-scanning method because then, I would be able to see the central topic or theme with its relationships with other sub-themes or ideas all in one single page. Idea-scan or mind-maps with my own symbols, icons and colours also serve as memory aids and guides. Use icons or symbols that are meaningful to you. When you are 'painting' or drawing symbols and icons in your idea map, think of the symbols and icons as an artist's palette.

Looking at Topic(s) From Various Angles

We can also think on our feet when we look at a particular topic from various angles.

Using our left brain we look at things, analysing them – looking at the different species or types, sizes, heights of individual trees in the forest. We are breaking down the whole elephant into parts. Using our right brain, we synthesise things. We are looking at the elephant as whole. We are looking at the big picture, looking at the forest rather than the individual trees. Using our values and feelings, we prefer some ways of doing things to others; we have our own preferences.

Analysing and Organising

Our talk or speech can also be looked at, analysed and organised in a number of ways.

Various methods or techniques exist and these include using the chronological (historical or time) order, comparing qualities and assessing the long or short-term measurements/ results or benefits (for instance, when arguing for the use of particular equipment versus another).

Thinking or recalling in an optimal order, that is, visualising chronologically is best especially when you are trying to think of a story or an event to relate.

Do look for examples to illustrate, nothing works better than examples and models.

One can also analyse and organises topics or ideas from simple to complex, starting from something easy, small to later more difficult and complex things or larger issue. There is a natural flow and it is relatively easy for your listeners to follow.

Next, we can also look at things in a concentric way. For example, take training, we can looking at training at the unit or departmental level, company level, and next, in terms of national, regional and then at the global level (that is, each time, we are looking at an even greater view). Such a way of thinking and organising offer the same excitement as the movements of a camera's zoom lens. The suspenseful, increasingly curiosity of discovering ever-greater or even ever-smaller views of the same reality. When do you use this technique? Use it whenever you want to exploit a suspenseful moment or avoid direct confrontation.

Further, we may want to evaluate the advantages and disadvantages (the pros and cons), and the strengths and weaknesses of an idea, a theory or practice. You can also play up to the advantages or load many benefits if you are selling a certain idea to people. Use 'you' and 'your' in your vocabulary as you sell the benefits. When you talk to others along this line, it appears logical and clear while appealing to their interests. Build momentum by starting with the least impressive or the most familiar thing your products, or idea does, then work up to the most exciting one as a climax. This technique can also be adapted, reversed to warn your listener about the downsides of a product, or idea; and save the worst for the last.

Look at Opposites

We can also assess idea(s) by looking at its antonyms. These are opposites and counterparts; examples include A & Z, male and female, Sun and Moon, arms and legs, full and empty, angel and Satan, shallow and deep, lost and found, clever and stupid, fresh and stale, fresh and canned, night and day, good and evil, yes and no, profit and loss, and up and down. More examples include black and white, learn and forget, high and low, quick and slow, fears and hopes, classical and jazz, clean and dirty, union and management, old versus new economy, and a host of others. Indeed, the examples can be endless. What we are doing is practising reverse thinking. Instead of looking at "shortage of staff" now, we look from the angle of "excess work". When you reverse the way you look at a particular subject, you would actually see new relationships.

Yet another example is that of looking at a particular topic not only from the Western viewpoints but also from the Eastern perspectives. We can look at the Yin and Yang of things (a Taoist perspective), the two opposing principles of the universe – the male and female energies. These dualities constitute the Taoist understanding of the cosmos and can be used to describe or analyse phenomena or issues with which we are familiar. Foods also contain the yin-yang elements. One Singapore newspaper once carried an article that spoke of "what's cool and what's not". "Heaty" food like mutton, ginger "raises your body temperature and improves your blood circulation". "Cooling" food hydrates your body" and examples include Lotus roots, Chinese pear and Winter melon. (The Sunday Times, 20 Feb 2000, p. 7). And indeed, a balanced diet should contain proper amounts of yin and yang. Look at Chinese art, medicine, and science, yin-yang pervades. In Chinese art, for example, the mountains are the yang while the valleys and streams are yin.

In fact, when you set-up opposites or reversals for your listeners, you will communicate quickly and clearly. Use such opposites in hard-edged situations that call for dramatic contrast.

A variant to thinking and setting up "opposites" is that of "contrarian" thinking. Here, we would think and go against the trend(s). We think and move to avoid the crowd or the herd instincts. What's current and fashionable, we'll avoid. When the majority buy, we then sell. When they sell, we buy. Or we become the first to try what others have not done or dare to do. Doing something different, daring to be the first always brings much excitement though it involves some risks. And this thinking and efforts may bring in rewards.

Have you ever pondered why it is that some people seem to have the ability to rise or soar in their careers? Low (2013) spoke of being **MAD: Make A Difference** for oneself and be able to market oneself, and grow one's career. One can truly stand for one's values espoused. One can also, for example, believe in quality; one then does one's work with pride. And indeed so, one embraces and practices the value of continuous improvement, and gains the edge. This is also in line with Total Quality Management (TQM); one keeps on improving; moreover, new ideas and improvements make work interesting.

He also highlighted the need to be positive to be different. "Avoid negative thinking… There is a need to turn on the GREEN LIGHTS in our lives. In this world, there are many pessimists and people who think negatively. And they look at the bad or unhelpful perspective of things… … to think positively is equal to Okawa's (2003) Invincible Thinking. Life, like building a tunnel, appears often blocked by solid rock but when one thinks positively, one sees the light. One fires oneself up and one proceeds, step by step, and makes progress. Trials and problems build us up, and we grow; they indeed toughen us." (Low, 2013: 502-503).

Of Likes and Twins

And yes, we can also assess idea(s) by looking at its synonyms (same meanings or allegorical, similar to picture words). We can also think of pictures words, words that paint images in your listeners' mind. Such words put pictures in your listeners' mind. Examples of some pictures that you may find insightful include:

On experience and outside help: A consultant is like a doctor for business.

Of no substance: All sizzle, no steak!

On fruitless attempt: Nailing jelly to the wall

On cover-ups: You can dress-up a dog, but its tail will stick out.

Of Cause and Effect

Also, we can look at a particular topic or theme in terms of its cause and effect – What it is and how it works. One thing or event happens and it leads to another. A leads to B, and then, C happens. The domino effect? Here, we are looking at the causal relationship.

Be a Journalist

Next, we should note that a journalist – often reporting on news for broadcast, print or online media – is out in the field chasing news and following up on tips and leads.

Here, we can apply the 5Ws & 1H or the so-called journalistic approach, i.e. looking at Who, What, Where, When, Why and How. This is excellent when drafting brochures, pamphlets, or when giving clear instructions. This will help you pull information together without leaving any important things out.

Be a Diplomat

Additionally, to think on our feet, the diplomatic approach can also be resorted to. In office life, we need to frequently manage conflicts, and one such way is to use the diplomatic approach. You may disagree about principles or on certain points raised by others and you may spend much time persuading others to act in ways that fit your plans. We tackle or attack issues, and not the person. And hence, we use positive language to convey a willingness to

17

help. Supervisors or office colleagues may have made the "wrong decision" but you are more likely to change their minds if you resort to "Perhaps, some other options may exist and we need to think about them". Other examples include: instead of saying, "Tell me how to handle it", we may say, "Let us discuss on ways to handle this." Instead of saying, "Never forget", say, "Do remember". And say, "I will do something for you" instead of "I can't do anything more for you". Basically, what we need to do is to turn the negative concepts frequently imbedded in our sentences into positive ideas.

There is, however, a caveat in this diplomatic approach. We must not let positive words grow into euphemisms that hide the truth. You may say, "You are working, but you really need to work harder" instead of "You are lazy". But don't say, "You are temporarily affected by non-action. O! Great, you really have unhurried charms."

Be Funny

Have humour; laughter is said to be the best medicine.

Rutus Wainwright once said these, "There's no life without humour. It can make the wonderful moments of life truly glorious, and it can make tragic moments bearable."

Do relate a funny story or tell a joke. You can also use humour to think on your feet, looking at the funny side of things. Look at the lighter side of things.

Life Cycle, Economic Cycle & Cycle of Things

There are often ups and downs, and we can also look at the cycle of things. Interestingly, nature always follows a cycle. Things are not a constant. Everything in Nature operates and goes through a cycle. There are seasons, times, spells and reasons for things. According to Buddhism, and Hinduism, life is a cycle – after birth, growth, maturity, sickness and death. In management too, it can be seen as a cycle of planning, organising, implementing and tracking or reviewing performance from time to time. All businesses also go through cycles – rags to riches, riches to poor; there are economic cycles of recession, depression, recovery and inflation.

Cultivate cyclical thinking. Think along virtuous cycle, gain a win-win situation and avoid vicious cycle. A vicious cycle can be like hatred that in turn creates more hatred, disagreements and wars. Hatred will not remove hatred. Two wrongs do not make a right. Force will not remove force. Think of virtuous cycle, love and compassion generates more love, benevolence and peace. Love dissolves hatred.

S.C.R.E.A.M.

Would you also prefer to **S.C.R.E.A.M.** to evoke ideas thinking on your feet? I prefer to use mnemonics (pronounced *knee-mon-nics*), techniques used to remember things, helping us thinking on our feet; hence the word – "**S.C.R.E.A.M.**"

Yes, here, S is to think of SUBSTITUTES for certain ingredients, materials, parts, places, people, uses or functions. Even, do ask what procedures can be substituted? US First Lady Hillary Clinton is known to hold imaginary conversations with Mahatma Gandhi and the former First Lady Eleanor Roosevelt. In some situations, she would ask herself and think, for example, what Gandhi would have done. She is substituting Gandhi for herself and we can do it too.

C means thinking of COMBINING the functions or uses, creating an assortment of things or ideas. The 3-in-1 instant coffee, tea, and Milo are all old products but thought of with a new twist, combining and packing the sugar, milk powder and the coffee/ tea/ Milo to the sachet. Varying combinations of four tastes – sweet, sour, bitter and salty – create the food flavours you enjoy or dislike.

The art, some even say the heart, of thinking creatively on your feet is combination. Creative thoughts and "solutions" don't just happen; they come from things that exist. A colour television, for example, appears to have hundreds of colours yet the images you see are combinations of just three colours. This art of combination is, in fact, well put by Dales Carnegie when he stated that "the ideas I stand for are not mine. I borrowed them from Socrates. I swiped them from Chesterfield. I stole them from Jesus. And I put them in a book".

And R is to think of REARRANGING the order or sequence, coming up and presenting with something new. Perhaps, you can think of rearranging the schedule or timetable or sequence of presenting the events, ideas or topics.

E is to ELIMINATE, ask ourselves what can be omitted or deleted. What can I understate or ignore to present something else? You can think of eliminating procedures, streamlining processes or looking at effective ways of doing things. Eliminate or stunt the growth of certain trees and voila, we have bonsai trees.

And next, we can also ask what we can ADAPT, that is, A. Adapting means asking and thinking whether any ideas from the past can be used or brought back. What other things resemble this? Can we develop new products from old or existing products? Can we use ideas from other fields or industries?

A good example of ADAPTING is the use of dogs. Dogs, man's best friend, have been adapted to help guide the blind. Also, dogs have also been adapted for military defence. These war dogs were selected, and trained by the American troops to sensing out traps as well as saving lives during the Vietnam War.

Finally the M in **S.C.R.E.A.M.** means MAGNIFY or MODIFY – what can be enlarged or extended, looking and thinking at that particular project or thing with a larger, higher, longer or broader view. Can you look at it and say you could multiply it? This MAGNIFY thinking method can be seen as similar to that of concentric technique, our mind is like a camera that zooms and sees the object larger and larger.

In the MODIFY thinking technique, one example is Disneyland's modification of the usual job titles and descriptions. In this way, its new members are introduced to Disneyland's own unique language and tradition. Customers are "guests", cleaners are "custodians" and employees are "cast members" who when on duty are "on stage".

We can also borrow Edward De Bono's Six Thinking Hats as a framework for on-the-spot thinking. To me, De Bono presents a simple but effective way to become a better thinker. He interestingly separates thinking into six distinct types, identifying six coloured "thinking hats". When dealing with:

1 — facts, figures, and objective information, use the White hat thinking
2 — emotions and feelings, apply the Red hat thinking
3 — logical negative thoughts, use the Black hat thinking
4 — positive constructive thoughts, use the Yellow hat thinking
5 — creativity and new ideas, apply the Green hat thinking
6 — control of the other hats and thinking steps, apply the Blue hat thinking ways.

Simply put, "putting on" a hat focuses our thinking; "switching" hats redirects thinking. With the different parts of the thinking process thus clearly defined, our communications and discussions with others can have better focuses and be more productive.

Knowing all the above techniques do help a lot in your thinking on your feet. As Aristotle once said that "memory is a habit which will make a man readier in reasoning", memorise and adopt these techniques as your thinking habits. Indeed, they will make you an agile thinker, enabling you to think strategically. It is like swimming or riding a bike. Once you have mastered it, you just do it. You do not think about swimming or riding a bike, you just do it. Your thinking habits are very much just like this too. Interestingly, mastering these techniques can also help you a lot in thinking creatively looking at a particular topic or issue from many and different perspectives.

Like what Prof. Osheroff, Nobel Laureate, (nickname "The Brain" while in school) has highlighted on his tips for success (The Straits Times, 24 Feb 2000, p. 45), we can also apply these – getting our hands dirty, "hav(ing) a good technical background, being curious, and "find(ing) out how things work" so that in widening our horizons, we can creatively think from a multitude of perspectives.

In your speeches and presentations should you go dry up, don't panic? Invite and ask for questions. Pause and compose yourself – make it look like a natural break. Then start off on another point.

Use our imagination. Imagine a little. Stretch a little. Change a little. Everyone is creative in some ways and we can think well on our feet – after all, "imagination is more important than knowledge" (Albert Einstein).

Indeed so, thinking on your feet and creatively is also critical during negotiations. "Skill at inventing solutions is one of the most useful assets a negotiator can have. A creative option can often make the difference between deadlock and agreement" (Roger Fisher and William Ury).

****

"A single idea if it is right, saves us the labour of an infinity of experiences!"

Jacques Maritain

****

AH SENG GOES TO HEAVEN

Ah Seng dies and goes to Heaven and St. Peter himself meets him at the Pearly Gates. The gates are closed, however, and Ah Seng approaches the gatekeeper. St. Peter says, "Aaaah, Ah Seng, it's certainly good to see you."

St. Peter then continued, "We have heard so many good things about you. I must inform you that the place is filling up fast, and we've been giving an entrance quiz for everyone.

The tests are short, but you need to pass before you can enter Heaven."

Ah Seng responds "It sure is good to be here, St. Peter. I was looking forward to this. Nobody ever told me about any entrance exam. Sure hope the test not so hard; life was a big enough test as it was." St. Peter then replies, "I know, Ah Seng, but the test is only three questions:

"What days of the week begin with the letter T?"

"How many seconds are there in a year?"

"What is God's first name?"

Ah Seng goes away to think the questions over. He returns the next day and goes to St. Peter to try to answer the questions.

St.Peter waves him up and says, "Now that you have had a chance to think the questions over, tell me your answers".

Ah Seng replies, "Okay, the first one, how many days of the week begin with the letter "T"?" "Shucks, that one's easy. That'd be Today and Tomorrow."

The Saint's eyes open wide and he exclaims, "Ah Seng! It's not what I was thinking, but... you do have a point though, and I guess I didn't specify, so I will give you credit for that answer. How about the next one?"

"How many seconds in a yeah (year)? Now that one's harder" says Ah Seng, "but I thought and thought about that and I guess the only answer can be twelve."

Astounded, St. Peter says "Twelve! Twelve! Ah Seng, how in Heaven's name could you come up with twelve seconds in a year?"

Ah Seng says "Aw, come on, St. Peter, it has to be twelve, January second, February second, March second..."

"Hold it" interrupts St. Peter. "I see where you're going with it. I see your point, though that wasn't quite what I had in mind, but I'll give you credit for that one too. Let's go on with the next and final question. Can you tell me God's first name?"

Ah Seng replies, "Andy." When St. Peter asked how in the world he came up with the name Andy, Ah Seng replies, "You know, St. Peter, that song we sing in church:

"Andy (and He) walks with me, Andy (and He) talks with me."

The moral of the story: THERE IS ALWAYS ANOTHER POINT OF VIEW, and just because another person doesn't see things the same way or understand the same way that you do, does not mean that it's wrong.

There is always another angle to see and present.

<u>Source</u>: The Biggest Joke Book Ever by: Jack Jacoby

Your Notes, Ideas
& Action Points

Chapter 3

Preventive Thinking & Getting Ahead In Your Career

"Dig a well before you thirst."
A Chinese Saying

"Prevention is better than cure
Reduces the stress you need endure."
Dick McCann and Jan Stewart (1997)

Dick McCann and Jan Stewart (1997) relate the story of how a young frog so excited to find a new home had selected "this wonderful billabong, where there was no-one else living. It was surrounded by large trees which let their branches dip into the water. Indeed, he was enchanted." He and the other frogs could set their home without interference from the any of the older frogs. He convinced the other young frogs to go to this new Promised Land and off they went. They arrived and were delighted to find a place of their dream. Immediately, they jumped into the water and looked at all the banks for comfortable places where they could live. "Within twelve hours they were all asleep, never to be awaken again. No one had thought to ask why the pond was uninhabited. Effluent from the chemical factory further up the creek contained poisonous chemicals which had polluted the pond, killing all previous inhabitants. Had the young frog and his friends investigated further, they would have seen that the trees were dying and their branches were dipping into the pond as they wilted. The water was mysterious, misty blue".

'A Stitch in Time Saves Nine'

Remember this English proverb? Or another, 'prevention is better than cure'. We need to look before we leap. Preventive thinking is critical, preventing us from sliding down. To prevent means to avoid, ward off or take steps avoiding an ugly situation or something that we don't want happening to us.

Even when change occurs, don't be a falling star; and stay in the game – you need to be that still valued high potential employee. Remember what was important and regarded as number one priority, may no longer apply today. Know the shifting priorities; know the players. Know what is acceptable in the old order may not be so in the new order. Be prepared to accept and adapt to new challenges. At the same time, we need to know the rules of what are acceptable behaviours. Knowledge of the unwritten rules – from dress code to management style of the new order – help. Keep afloat; know what is important. Find out more from older colleagues who have been around longer. These help us to avoid later surprises or disappointments. Know the people who can help or further your career and those who could hinder you. Foster your relationships with the '*friendlies*' while avoiding the ones who are in competition with you.

These aside, Dick McCann and Jan Stewart (1997) offer these guidelines and tips for managers with frog-like tendencies "who forget the age-old advice to 'look before they leap'". Accordingly, "in the short term, (the authors advises to) use the 5WH technique (5W questions and one H (how question) when faced with a decision(, that is, ask yourself):

O What information do you need?
O Why do you need it?
O Where will you get it from?
O Who will get it?

O   When do you need it?
O   How will you get it?"

And in the longer term, we need to "get into the habit of:

O   Setting aside time to read, research and be aware of the latest developments in the field.
O   Allocating time to meet with others to learn what they are thinking and planning.
O   Considering what information you should share with others to foster a good information flow.
O   Consulting key stakeholders on any projects to ensure that their concerns and ideas are taken into account before any decisions are made."

When we do preventive thinking, we are better prepared. We see possibilities, seize opportunities and become more adaptable. When we do preventive thinking, we daringly face with whatever challenges posed. And the impossible becomes possible; nothing is impossible!

Preparing Your Parachute

– Getting Ahead in Our Jobs

We have our jobs; we also need to strategise, avoid being fired! Perhaps, here are just some ideas to set you thinking conversely and preventatively. Just think of what must we do to get fired; and these can include:

O   Produce little.
O   Do non-essential things
O   Badmouth the company
O   Accept little responsibilities - pass the buck, etc.
O   Be a trouble maker
O   Blame others

O   Obstruct, if not, refuse to carrying out the work as instructed.
O   Act lazy on the job
O   Be absent and late for work frequently.
O   Show no or little interest in the work
O   Show bad attitude
O   Don't give a damn to service quality.
O   Mislead customers
O   Be rude to customers.

Understanding the most basic climbing tools can help us move ahead in our careers. Some of the researches I have done show what successful people do to be memorable, credible, successful and trusted are:

Adopting Various Strategies in Learning to Love Your Work

Love the work. Get some fun out of your work. Work is fun when it is done well. Tailor your job to your psychic needs. Ensure that your values match, in most ways, to that of your company. Of course, this does not mean that you approve of or believe in everything the company does, but it does mean – You generally believe in, if not admire, its policies and economic legitimacy.

Also, do treasure the times that you have distinguished yourself. Look at your achievements; take pride, as they are your satisfactions of life.

Being and Staying Focused

Always have an aim. Realise the power of focusing. As Basil H. Linddell Hart conclusively agreed with Clausewitz, "the principles of war (*strategy, mine*), not merely one principle, can be condensed into a single word – '***concentration***'." Being focused helps determine much of what we get. Indeed, we can use the power of focus for the best or the worst. "A man's life is what thoughts (*being focused*) make of it." (Marcus Aurelius; added in *italics*, mine).

Think of a place you know well. You can focus on its good or bad aspects. Chances are and it is highly likely that what you focus on influences your mood. The way we focus on things everyday shapes our outlook in life. By being focused, we can impact and change our world; we change our lives too.

"Ask what you really want. Then focus" urges Dr. Mohd. Effendy, senior fire officer with Petrochemical Corporation of Singapore. "Asking and knowing what he wanted gave Dr. Effendy focus. He knew his future rested in further education." (The Straits Times, 5 Mar 2000, p. 15). And a university don once told me, "Look forward. Work hard and aim to be the best in your field – you'll be an expert in that field."

When you are focused, you set priorities. You could focus all your energies on what you hope to achieve. And achieve it!

Understanding the Bosses' Needs

A lot of people fail because they are not aware of what their bosses want. Understanding the bosses' needs is critical to career success. If you ignore the boss's needs and wants, you just might get fired. Very simply, you need to ask to understand the boss(es) and what (s)he or others around him or her value. You need to learn if (s)he likes dates such as when you finish what tasks, and whether (s)he needs to be supplied with the specifics. And what next and when. And on and on.

Most bosses want results – the quicker the better and (s)he is usually busy or have no time to get things done. And when (s)he wants information, (s)he wants them fast. (S)he may ask: "What's happening now?" or "What have you found out?" You need to get straight to the point. Know his or her priorities and deadlines.

Ask yourself: What is important to the boss? It is basic. Understanding the boss indeed gives you clarity and confidence.

Indeed, understand the boss well. If your boss is an extrovert/ activist while you tend to do more reflections and thinking, get back to him fast. Inform him or her of your progress. Otherwise, he may perceive you as rather slow or worse, passive in getting things done. Conversely, if you are an extrovert and your boss's an introvert, getting back quickly may lead him or her to perceive you as getting things done rather fast but without much reflection or thinking.

Next, don't just do the J.O.B., that is, **J**UST **O**BEY **B**OSS, with unquestioning and mindless obedience; or just follow instructions. But, do pro-actively fill an unmet need in the organisation. Be perceptive enough to recognise the organisation's unmet need(s). Create a new product for the company to expand its products and services. Hit on an idea, collect donated reading materials, set up a mini-library or a resource centre to serve the needs of the departmental staff. Organise the company's much needed recreational activities. Or do whatever to promote some form of camaraderie among your people.

Better still, run the department or unit as if you own the business. Monitor and cut costs, raise profits. Keep abreast of the competition. Take personal interest in all instances of customer dissatisfaction, and look at ways to better customer services. You'll gain an edge by running your operation as if you were the owner. "You are your own boss. If you fully embrace this approach to your work, you will derive pleasure in the prosperity of your 'business' and develop your talents to unforeseen heights… the value of our work lies not in the kind of position we hold but in the attitude we take on the job." (PHP/ Matsushita Konosuke, 1994: 69)

Avoiding that Bad "Catty" Habits

Here, McCannn, Dick and Stewart, Jan (1997) highlights that "many Cat managers consider that people are inherently lazy and incompetent and need constant supervision; otherwise they will not do a job well. They manage by fear, constantly waiting to pounce on anybody not working to the rules. When they want to 'play', then it is always on their terms and at a time that suits them. Cat managers can demotivate staff and decrease efficiency by creating a negative environment where people put energy into avoidance behaviours.

So much time is spent protecting their backside, that eventually the work environment becomes an unhappy place and productivity declines". They warn that "your team's respect (for you) will wither and die if you continually pounce, dominate and pry".

In avoiding to be Cat managers, McCannn, Dick and Stewart, Jan (1997) advise managers, among other things, to:

O Say each day something positive and listen to their team members
O Discuss with their team members how they can devolve more responsibility to them
O Ask others if they are aloof (if so, then plan to spend more time interacting positively with the team)
O "Review the balance between the technical and managerial aspects of (their) job(s)".

Getting Things Done

People who are selected, valued, and they who get ahead are those who produce results. They show their ability to get results. They do the job, getting things done. Bosses know that they get things done by their ways or pattern of productively identifying opportunities/ problems, thinking through, and offering solutions/ suggestions and acting to resolve problems.

Your company employs you. Always ask yourself: Have *you* a solution or are *you* part of the problem?

Tenacity

Keep going until something stops you. Tenacity is not giving up – it's keeping to your path. In life, we will receive setbacks, much discouragement and it will continue. But that's life – you have to be tenacious. Salespeople are taught that they need to hear many no's before it really might mean no for a customer. Those who persevere will succeed.

Related to tenacity is the need to fight the fear of failure. It is the efforts and determination to succeed that count too. Well, even if we fail, we learn and move on, and in fact, daringly too! "We need to feel comfortable that it's okay to fail. Failure is okay, fear is not. Fear will not help us create new things" as argued by Mr. Kamran Elahian, a member of the Technopreneurship Ministerial Committee (T21) International Resource Panel (The Straits Times, 6 Mar 2000, p. 4).

Having Peace of Mind

Confucius is reputed to have said this, "If looking within one's heart, one finds no cause for self-reproach, why should he worry, what shall he fear?" And an old Chinese tale tells of an artist who was so skilful that he painted a snake that looked so lifelike that the viewer might expect it to jump out of the picture. He got carried away and painted feet on the snake. This expression, "painting feet on the snake," has become a Chinese adage, referring to situations that are made more complicated than they need to be. We can be happier people if we reduce our anxieties and complexities of our lives.

Keep it simple. This is less stressful.

What we really need is the combined genius of getting things done, achieving them and not being anxious or having doubts about it! We have done the best that we can, that's it! Cut your losses! As for the rest, just go with the flow. Leave it to the natural scheme of things. And go about doing your daily activities in a normal way. Indeed, tensions reduced; and we can concentrate better on more productive endeavours.

Having Good Chemistry with People

Good chemistry also comes to someone who listens, learns and relates well with a good sense of humour. A fitting of values and of the same wavelength must exist between you and the top bosses. Being on the same wavelength makes people who work with you like you.

Even then, what is paramount is that you must deliver. Don't be too busy planning your career that you don't get today's job done.

Being Pro-active

Being arm-folded and not pro-active can lead you to little progress or growth and less profits. In fact, if you don't do more, you'll be committing a career suicide! Any exceptional talent you have will be wasted, if not, undeveloped. And you are likely not to receive more pay because you don't deserve more!

Be pro-active. "Work harder than everyone else" advises McCormack Mark. H. (1995, 1996). Always give the baker's dozen, do more than what the next person does. The secrets of success is in doing more, and smartly. You are seldom fired for doing too much. I prefer this approach, as you would then have less time to get involved in office politics or other problems. Besides, you become your own boss telling yourself what to do irrespective the chain of command.

"The surest sign of a leader is his or her ability to say, 'Do it now!' and it gets done." (McCormack Mark. H.; 1995, 1996). Pro-active people are the ones who get ahead. They are enterprising; they enliven their work. They go the second mile, turning goals into action plans. Write down what you plan to do, how, by whom and by when. Ummmph! Get several balls up in the air, be multi-dimensional and keep moving. Your actions best indicate your thoughts, making the people around you read you well.

Be enthusiastic! As Carl Jung put it, "There can be no transforming of darkness into light and of apathy into movement without emotion."

And to be in action and always producing results, do hire someone who is smarter than you – that way you keep yourself on your toes.

Being Flexible

Flexibility can be yet another success factor or strength of yours. And there is no one road through any problem or up any mountain.

You have to be effective dealing with suppliers, as you are effective dealing with the customer. You are effective in dealing with things, as you are effective in dealing with people. Also, display a positive attitude towards change; and respond positively to it. Change is, after all, an essential characteristic in today's work place.

Setting a Good Example for Others

Another good climbing tool is to win your co-workers by being an exemplar of how to conduct oneself in the workplace. Get noticed and be visible in a positive way. Gain the edge by being a good team leader and player by being helpful to those in need. And appeal to your co-workers' personal interests. Also, do obtain professional recognition to put yourself in good stead. Continuously update yourself.

> "Concentrate on
> a specific job,
> give your heart, soul
> and 100 per cent."
>
> Lim Bee Huat,
> Kopi Tiam King

Susan Long (1999) <u>Grit Success: Stories of Millionaires in Our Neighbourhood</u>, Singapore, Prentice Hall

Being Noticed by Top Management

When you set an example out of yourself, you get yourself noticed by the higher-ups or top management. Suggest ways to achieve the corporate goals. And make suggestions to cut the company's overall costs. In fact, the higher-ups usually appreciate any activity of people down the organisation that helps goal attainment.

Another technique is that of being mentioned in the company newsletters. Write or contribute to your corporate newsletter. Or do something fantastic or outstanding. If you achieve anything newsworthy such as winning an award, or whatever accomplishments, contact the company newsletter's editor. Being mentioned is an effective attention-getter because your name or even photographs in print are impressive. Anything, that is basically positive, works.

Learning

Simple question that makes a difference! Anthony Robbins speaks of Leo Buscaglia. "When he was young, Leo's father asked him every night, "**What have you learned today**?" The boy knew he had to have an answer – and a good one. If he hadn't learned anything interesting in school that day, he'd scurry for the encyclopaedia. Decades later, Leo still won't go to bed until he's learned something new and valuable for the day.

How could your life or your children's lives be immeasurably enhanced by adding this question, or one like it, to daily routine? In what ways could you make this process as fundamental as eating or sleeping?"

Keep questioning! Be hungry like a child for new experiences. Ask yourself if your present skills up to mark to achieve your future goals. Ask what you need to do to perform better. Initiate openings to acquire information or training.

Indeed, "old men are always young enough to learn, with profit." (AESCHYLUS, *Agamemnon*). Philip Yeo, chairman of the Economic Development Board (EDB) and "the man behind who makes billion-dollar bets" is still "learn(ing)", "cannot resist a new challenge when he sees one" and while many men his age are playing golf, he is studying…"(The Straits Times, 19 Feb 2000, p. 62 - 63). Learning helps – you are secure in yourself yet constantly improving.

Learning gives us choices and options; it helps to open more doors.

"Among other things, he (Philip Yeo) pushed a manufacturing company to go from bullets to semiconductors, got a shipping firm to branch into the bakery business and sprang the idea of building an island for new industry" (The Straits Times, 19 Feb 2000, p. 62).

Organisations need to be organic in preparing for the 21st. century. Corporate leaders and managers should be planning and preparing for change. They can also build organisations into self-organising teams ever ready to adapt to whatever opportunities emerge.

The country's wealth is its learning, working people. Knowledge produces wealth too. Would we not have a double-barrelled gun when we marry the two?

Suppose we pursue the flexibility and self-organisation by way of self-managing teams, are there not limits? Many flexible, information-driven companies can be too hasty to jump at superficially attractive market opportunities that their cool rivals smartly avoid. Teams have its place. However, for all its greatness, teams can at times be a many-headed beast. Teams at times cannot entirely manage themselves. The mix of fast-growing entrepreneurial outfits and smart, mobile, ambitious workers creates a workplace that can actually be more fragile than its industrial predecessors. In fact, solutions to work problems are more likely to come from good leaders (guiding flexible workers) than from the teams themselves.

According to Hout, most businesses do not move so fast that foresight, commitment, pre-emption, deterrence, and other traditional strategic elements no longer build business value. Even in the fastest industries, good managers can still add value by creating the right working atmosphere to spur creativity and innovation. In my opinion, leadership with an adaptable workforce matters most, more so in knowledge-based economy.

The Republic of Singapore's national leaders are urging us to develop:

(a) ourselves, learning for skills, life and living.
(b) as a world-class workforce in Singapore in the 21st century.
(c) a culture of learning, creativity, innovation, risk taking, technology and entrepreneurship. Hi-tech start-ups and technopreneurship are encouraged.

To achieve these, we can start first of all by being a strategic thinker. Welcome the change and take it as a challenge. We need to simply be adaptable, train and re-train ourselves where necessary. Do not be afraid to learn new things, update and upgrade. And companies should value the workers' intellectual and knowledge assets.

Don't ever postpone learning and upgrading. We all know that whenever it comes to exercising, we tend to say: 'Whenever the need comes, I'll do. And when the needs really come, I lie down for a while, just a while and it passes.'

These days with e-learning, there are no excuses. There are virtual institutes to promote learning. "E-learning is appealing concept because it allows people to receive training anytime and at any place. It is especially useful for those who wish to take up part-time courses after work to upgrade themselves" (*Virtual Institute to Promote e-learning* in <u>The Straits Times</u>, 5 Mar 2000, p. 1)

Workers and union members must believe in learning and empower themselves. Singaporeans will indeed lose our edge if we lose this value of being adaptable, learning and re-learning. "My people are destroyed for lack of knowledge." (Bible, *Hosea* 4:6).

There is a saying that goes: 'a little learning is a dangerous thing' but to this, we must add Twain's words: "training is everything. The peach was once a bitter almond; cauliflower is nothing but a cabbage with a college education."

Your Notes, Ideas
& Action Points

Chapter 4

Strategic Leadership Thinking and Insights from Some Chinese War Strategies

Strategy is the way of a general.
"Never interrupt your enemy when he is making a
mistake."

(Napoléon Bonaparte)

In this concise yet poignant chapter, looking at several Chinese war strategies of Ancient China [although there are many], the academic-practitioners seek to gather key lessons of strategic leadership thinking. One such key strategic thinking lesson, for example, is that it is better not to have any war at all, and that (peace and non-violence) is the greatest victory (win-win) for all. These success principles can in fact be applied not only in the battlefield but also in one's daily dealings and life at the workplace. Such wise understanding will not only increase one's ability to respond to problems, but also, be victorious in one's life, mission and responsibilities while having invaluable peace of mind.

Introduction

Why should one take a look at several of these Chinese war strategies? Books on the art of war, for example, Sun Tzu's and the

100 Strategies of War, take up an important position in traditional Chinese culture. (*100 Strategies of War* was written during the Song Dynasty, a few years after Sun Tzu's *Art of War*.) These books' rich, extensive and deep philosophy is highly acclaimed, and interestingly, military thinking not only sums up and directs the thousands of earth-shaking wars in the history of China, but has also influenced the growth of Chinese military affairs, literature and technology. After all, when it comes to strategy, why not apply what Confucius (Goodreads, 2014, cited in Low and Teo, 2014) urged, that is, "study the past if you would define the future.". Besides, war strategies can also be applied to business strategies to counter competition, increase market share and/or enhance business growth.

Chapter Aims and Objectives

Many war strategies and leadership lessons exist and there is, in fact, much to discuss by merely looking at several Chinese war strategies; it is the intention of this review research paper to draw out and analyse, what are, to the authors, as the vital and most preferred, if not, ten (10) best lessons of leadership from these war strategies. It is also hoped that these ten (10) principles for success can be applied not only in the battlefield but also in our business and everyday dealings. The paper is also about the art of advantage and maximising opportunity; this wisdom will increase one's ability to respond to problems, and be victorious in one's life and undertakings while having peace of mind. Moreover, "the essence of strategy is choosing what not to do (**and avoid**)" (Michael Porter, Goodreads, 2014, cited in Low and Teo, 2014, **bold**, authors' words) and succeed.

What Is Strategic Leadership?

"Strong leaders are an organisation's most vital resource." (Krause, 1997: 22). "Leadership in organisations is the process of guiding and directing the behaviour of people in the work environment" (Quick and Nelson, 2013: 380); "leadership is influence" (Maxwell, 1993:

1; Low, 2013a) and (getting followers,) leaders achieve goals and get results through people. They get people to "buy into" them before they "buy into" their leadership (Maxwell, 1993: 119). The people are with them; strategic leadership can thus be understood to give the vision, direction and ways or avenues to change or adapt for the growth and success of an organization.

The Merriam-Webster Dictionary (2014, cited in Low and Teo, 2014) defines "strategic" as "(1) of or relating to a general plan that is created to achieve a goal in war, politics, etc., usually over a long period of time" and "(2) useful or important in achieving a plan or strategy". Here, because of long-term thinking, being strategic can also be said to show or signify the sensibility, wisdom and acumen of the leader in attaining the plan or strategy.

1   The Soldiers' (People's) Vital Trust in the Commander/ leader

Trust is beyond price; trust is priceless. Trust influences a leader's impact and the company's bottom line or results more than any other single thing.

Among all the qualities of the greatest leaders of our time, one stands above the rest: These leaders are all highly trusted. One can have a compelling vision, rock-solid strategy, excellent communication skills, innovative insight, and a skilled team, but if people don't trust the leader, one will never get the results one wants (Horsager, 2012).

During the Spring and Autumn Period, Duke Wen of Jin surrounded the kingdom of Yuan and predicted that the battle would end within three days. In spite of his General's advice to attack one more time so that Yuan surrender, he resisted after all, his people were ready to go home to meet their family members and loved ones. They had in the first place agreed to end the battle in three days; it was time to disperse the army then. Had he gained the kingdom of Yuan, he would lose the people's trust and this he cannot bear; he was more concerned with what can he protect his people with? For Duke Wen, the people's trust, a precious commodity, was indeed too great to be sacrificed for something small – even if another kingdom was won.

Besides, because the general did not fear death, so also were the soldiers, and the leader's actions were exemplary. When fighting, soldiers must be prepared to die without fear or regret. If the top echelon can be trusted, the soldiers will give of their best without questioning. If the general (leader) is trustworthy, is just in instilling discipline and does not show favouritism, the entire army will be united against the enemy (the competition).

Trust cannot be built overnight; it really requires time, effort, diligence, character and consistency (Horsager, 2012). Krause (1997) spoke of the leader's example, strength of character and inner fortitude. Very simply, the key lesson here is that if the commander/ leader is trustworthy, the soldiers will have no hesitation in following his orders; they will even die for him. In war or in business, the trust of the people in the leader must prevail (Gagliardi, 2011); otherwise the leader will not be successful.

2   The Military Commander/ leader Should Be Flexible

Note that the opposite of flexibility is rigidity. Bertrand Russell 1872-1970, the English logician and philosopher once lamented (12Manage.com, 2014, cited in Low and Teo, 2014) that, "the whole problem with the world is that fools and fanatics are always so certain of themselves, but wiser people so full of doubts."

Herodotus, 5th century BC, Greek historian highlighted that, "unless a variety of opinions are laid before us, we have no opportunity of selection, but are bound of necessity to adopt the particular view which may have been brought forward" (12Manage.com, 2014, cited in Low and Teo, 2014), and this can indeed add to closing of doors, options and minds as well as much inflexibility. Rigidity, to the authors, means closed minds and lack of openness; there is indeed a lack of mind growth and failure to see possibilities and different perspectives. And Michaelson and Michaelson, 2010 and Michaelson (2001) argued that when one is rigid, one is predictable.

And he also indicated that in competitive encounters and crusades, predictability can be a weakness. Being predictable can signal one's proposed action(s) or move(s) to one's opponents, and the odds of failure increase.

"Victory is won by flexibly coping with circumstances" (Sun Tzu, translated by Zhang Huimin, cited in Michaelson, 2001: 57). To paraphrase Low (2010a)'s account of Sun Tzu, when leaders see the subtleties, they can easily win. When the leader plans, he is prepared. He needs to think of various possible settings and responses. He becomes agile of foot; he will not trip when the landscape changes, but will trot on regardless of rocks and obstacles. On even ground one will move swiftly, as fleet-footed as a deer in flight, and on steep rocky inclines, one will be as surefooted as a mountain goat.

To Sun Tzu, a Taoist, the leader should be like water; flexible (a kin of life, and if one becomes inflexible, one becomes a kin of death), (s)he adapts and moves well. To Lao Tzu, the highest good is like water; it gives life to the ten thousand beings and does not struggle. It flows in places men reject and so is like Tao.

Excellent Chinese military moves stress on being flexible, applying appropriate strategy depending on the situation and circumstances. They consider and vary their tactical options (Sun Tzu, mentioned in Michaelson and Michaelson, 2010; Michaelson, 2001). The military would emulate its desired flexibility like that of a dragon; when the competition attacks its head, the Chinese dragon uses its tail to strike. When its tail is attacked, it uses its head to strike the enemy. When the enemy attacks its center portion, both its head and tail will strike the enemy (Low, 2009: 55; 2010). There is truly wisdom in quick-wittedness, and mental agility is often cherished. First gets the oyster, and last gets the shell; good generals often respond or move their troops with lightning speed as those who delay will be on the defensive. Very much like putting a bottle of good wine at the finishing line, those who arrive first enjoy the drinks, and get drunk while those who come later could not even wet their lips. Whether in leadership or in marketing, there's much smartness, for example, in Singapore's hosting of Asia's first night Grand Prix, Formula One, reaping the publicity and benefits of the first mover (Low, 2008).

Flexible, the military commander needs to be adaptable whether the army is fighting whether in the marshes, on home ground, enemy ground or in a strategic location. The military commander can also find himself, at times, fighting in a desperate situation, or at times, in a dangerous situation. He should also learn how to handle a defeat well. Or for that matter, like the military commander, leaders should (learn how to) lead in any situation or, in fact, handle a crisis well.

In effecting strategy, flexibility is crucial; there are no single but a variety of solutions and options. Flexible and even creative human resource programme can also help to reduce staff turnover and various schemes and incentives may be adopted. And these among other things, include birthday leave, community service leave, grandparent leave, floating cultural day, outcome based employment contract, and many others, considering the local context as well as the competitive international environment.

3　The Military Commander Should Not Assume or Take Anything for Granted

Next, we will discuss one of the many strategies under the 36 military strategems, maxims that have become China's most revered sources of wisdom; they are ways of raising one's sphere of influence. One particular strategem is "to cross the river under camouflage", chosen because we should not assume the ordinary as ordinary or that anything can happen from the ordinary. Basically, the strategy highlights or alerts us that a recognisable or an obvious, everyday sight usually attracts no attention, and in fact can be taken for granted. The more ordinary the activity, the less attention it draws; it is thus said that secrets often hide in the open (Low, 2010a); thus, the usefulness of this strategy.

Fraudsters may sometime take advantage of such obvious everyday happenings such as working late (overtime) almost everyday or having long, accumulated leave periods while committing fraud and surreptitiously taking monies from the till. A key lesson for corporate leaders; indeed, they need to ensure that such things are not assumed or taken for granted. Checks and counter checks should be made to prevent misappropriations or frauds; at least, corporate leaders should not assume or take anything for granted. A good case in point has been highlighted by Low (2006: 66), that is, the famous February 1995 Barings debacle is, in fact, a classic 'lack of separate of duties' case, a feature that was assumed as **normal** in the company due to the busyness of the traders and the industry as a whole. Nick Leeson assumed multiple roles, wearing many hats. He was the General Manager, head trader and, due to his experience in operations, de facto head of the back office. Such an arrangement should have rung alarm bells, but no one within Barings' senior management appeared to **notice the blatant conflicts of interest; yet this was considered normal**. Accordingly, Leeson and his traders had usual authority to perform two types of trading, i.e., transacting futures and options orders for clients and for other firms within Barings, and arbitraging price differences between Nikkei futures traded on the SIMEX and Japan's Osaka exchange. In short, his wearing multiple hats easily allowed him to avoid detection (Leeson, 1997, Low, 2006, authors' emphasis in bold).

When things are obviously peaceful, all the more we need to take guard or be extra careful. And, in fact, be ever vigilant.

4 The Commander Should Embrace Humility and Conversely, Make the Enemy Feel Arrogant

At strategic level, changing or manoeuvring is a way of thinking about how one is going to act in a way that puts one's opponent at a disadvantage (Michaelson, 2001).

Low (2010a: 55) indicated that great wisdom is not obvious or shown, and great value is often not advertised; humility is also unbroken and an integral part of strategic leadership. And the military commander should not take things for granted. Or he should not be proud or arrogant. Instead he should be humble. When he is humble or modest, he can also take the strategy of making the other party or the rival feel arrogant or bloated with overconfidence. And the other party would underestimate or misread him.

If the enemy is strong, one may not be able to win the war. In this regard, it is wise to be modest when dealing with them. At the same time, offer them handsome gifts to flatter them and wait for an opportunity to attack.

Napoleon (cited in Goodreads, 2014, cited in Low and Teo, 2014) once said that, "Never interrupt your enemy when he is making a mistake." When one's enemy gets carried away, becomes complacent and is less alert, then this is the time to defeat the enemy. The rule or trick is that humility enables one to achieve success.

Since the olden days, even at ground level, arrogant soldiers have always been defeated. Even experienced warriors are no exception. Clever generals are not only humble but calm too. Composed, such a leader is better able to come up and devise plans to make the enemy feel big-headed, absorbed by self-importance and pride. In this way, victory is assured, and what is applicable to the opponent is similar to the English saying, "Pride comes before a fall".

5   The Commander Has A Clarity of Purpose and Vision

Sheldon Adelson highlighted that, "I've already figured out when I'm going to be No. 2 and No. 1" (afterQuotes, 2014, cited in Low and Teo, 2014).

Some people never see or lack the clarity; and they are the ever wanderers. The commander or the leader knows where (s)he is heading or wants to go to (Maxwell, 1993). The strategic leader also knows what he wants. One of the keys to leadership is to have priorities (Maxwell, 1993: 19-34) or to be precise, a clarity of one's priorities. It is also worthy to note that strategic leaders should know themselves. They know that they have the necessary passion and a zeal for work that goes beyond money and power. Besides, strategic leaders are inclined to achieve the vision and goals with much energy and intense determination (MSG, 2013; Krause, 1997).

Clarity is very important for the customers and stakeholders of the Company; "one of the things that is most important for a company is to be very clear about their strategy, so investors get to self-select as to whether or not that's the right strategy for them." (Jeff Bezos, cited in afterQuotes, 2014). Horsager (2012) also indicated that "people trust the clear and mistrust or distrust the ambiguous".

All in all, the leader definitely needs to be clear about his or her mission, purpose, expectations, and daily activities. When a leader is clear about expectations, (s)he will likely get what (s)he wants. When one is clear about priorities on a daily basis, one becomes productive and effective.

Moreover, a leader's actions, as the evidence of his or her clarity, must extend naturally from his or her understanding. When a leader is both clear and congruent, an organisation trusts in their judgment, in their capacity as a leader, in the course they've set and the decisions they've taken and this trust permeates their people's feelings, thoughts, and actions.

As a leader, one's clarity (or lack of it) is visible or noticeable in the way one perceives, thinks and acts. When one is clear, one knows what to look for - and what to watch out for. One has a reference point around which to organise one's thinking – to both spark and to manage one's creativity. And one knows precisely where, when, and how to act – congruently and confidently.

And in terms of strategic change and leadership, Healthfield (2014; in **bold**, authors' emphasis) concluded that "a lot of what I see regarding change, hasn't changed over the years... ...it's 'repackaged', replicated, improved upon, etc. Basically if you **define the objective**, train your people (give them the tools), **communicate at all levels expectations**, (Note: what's in it for me and rewards and recognition) and reward for success, change (and teams) will be successful."

6   The Commander Should Always Be Prepared – Do Due Preparations/ planning and then Wait

Close to the strategy of not taking anything for granted is to make due preparations, bearing in mind that "Rome wasn't built in a day".

Dwight D. Eisenhower, the United States' post-World War 2 president once stressed (Goodreads, 2014, cited in Low and Teo, 2014) that, "in preparing for battle I have always found that plans are useless, but planning is indispensable." When one is well prepared, one can concentrate on one's strengths and battles are truly won by focusing on one's strengths. Operations succeed because someone knows how to concentrate strengths against weaknesses. If one does not have clear or real superiority, one cannot win (Sun Tzu cited in Michaelson, 2001). When one is well prepared, one can indeed be confident, cool and calm; and one can ordinarily have the luxury of time, organising one's resources and/ or waiting to ambush or attack. One can choose when to attack.

Remember too the Boy Scouts' motto, "Be prepared", and this is very applicable in strategy. While humble or modest, the leader should be well prepared, and in being in state of preparations, the leader gains a lead time. In this connection, let us examine the Stratagem 4, that is, "Wait at ease for the fatigued enemy" (Low, 2010a). Resting may give the impression of being laidback and weak; however, it provides the leader with an opportunity to consolidate his strength(s). This can in fact be combined with the earlier principle #2 that the commanders should be flexible – what appears soft and pliable can be strong and solid. The supple bamboo yields to the wind and remains standing unlike the mighty oak bough that snaps or breaks.

Sun Tzu once said, "He who is better prepared... will win." "Decisions made without thinking are often expensive" (Krause, 1997: 42). Sun Tzu, *The Art of War*, spoke of those "who wishes to fight must first count the cost" (Goodreads, 2014, cited in Low and Teo, 2014) and this is part of preparations and planning. And Low

(2010a: 39, *italics ours*) has added that, "Yes, it (*preparations and planning*) can be tedious, but there is no substitute for it. Indeed, the power to win is nothing unless we have the power to prepare."

Good commanders are normally well-prepared and beforehand they would survey and factor-in the terrain; they normally would have done their homework before they attack or enter into battle.

Yet another angle of this strategy is that after one's homework and due preparations have been made, one has certainly marshalled all the information and resources. The successful strategic leader (a good negotiator-cum-influencer) has done a thorough strengths/ weaknesses/ opportunities and threats (SWOT) analysis of the other party (OP) and himself/his party. The leader is well prepared; persuasive, (s)he can better guide his or her people. The leader can be said to be influencing or persuading his or her people from a position of strength.

7   The Good Commander Ensures Good Strategic Maintenance

In leadership and good marketing, strategic maintenance is critical, if one keeps on improving, bit by bit (*kaizen* or continuous improvement is effected), one develops leadership excellence, and with that, rivals may find it difficult to shoot or down a moving target (Low, 2009a).

Ensuring good strategic maintenance, leaders relate well, "appreciat(ing) the gifts of (the) family" (Lonely Planet, 2011: 117, cited in Low, 2014) and making the people (organisational members/ citizens) part of the family (Low, 2014: 176). Note that people also want to have friends and connections (Horsager, 2012), and it is also helpful to maintain good relationships and understanding with people and others around us (Horsager, 2012; Krause, 1997). Horsager (2012) indeed pointed out that "grateful people are not entitled, they do not complain, and they do not gossip. (They) develop the trait of gratitude, and you (the strategic leader) will be a magnet". After all, as Sun Tzu pointed out (Goodreads, 2014, cited in Low and Teo,

2014), "when one treats (one's) people with benevolence, justice, and righteousness, and reposes confidence in them, the army will be united in mind and all will be happy to serve their leaders."

Today's leader is not someone who knows all the solutions or answers because in this world that is impossible. The new or strategic leader is "someone who can assess a situation, bring people together, build consensus and discover solutions, drawing on the talents of everyone involved. The new leader is a facilitator, a communicator, a team builder, who realizes that our greatest natural resources are our minds and hearts, together with those of the people, around us" (Dreher, 1996: 5).

Valuing people (Sun Tzu, cited in Gagliardi, 2011; Michaelson and Michaelson, 2010) as one's "most appreciable asset" (Maxwell, 1993: 113), a good commander and a strategic leader should take care of his or her people. And monitoring, maintaining and overall up-keeping of the people's trust is one good example of such strategic maintenance. Here, we should next examine stratagem 10 that speaks of "concealing a dagger in a smile" (Low, 2010a). This saying is similar to the, saying, "Have Buddha face but with tiger heart." True, a strategy is a strategy and a tactic is a tactic; it's thinking that makes it good or bad. However, if the intention is ethically unbecoming, then it should not be subscribed; the authors do not urge or even encourage leaders to adopt this strategy since they believe that leadership should be not be hypocritical but rather be run in a sincere way and plain honesty is indeed preferred. Leadership can even, what more, be applied with the Confucian character and integrity (*lien*) in mind.

Moreover, in the above strategy, on the surface or from the external appearance, the leader looks kind, but at heart (s)he is far from kind. (S)he may even have an untoward intention towards the people. It can also be taken as winning the people's trust and getting what one wants only after the people's guard is down. Or after winning the elections, the leader may not deliver the goods or even do what that has been promised. In other words, the leader is nice to the people, gaining their trust, while all the while setting them up to take the fall or loss. The leader can also, sometimes, put forward or cast the deal in a positive light to make the situation palatable, thus misleading the people. Indeed to stress, trust here is broken or not up-kept.

It should overall be noted that as leaders, one needs to take cognisance that this is really a short-term move or step; leaders and even friends need to ensure that others' trust of them is not misplaced or lost, and should, in fact, be always there. The leader's maintains his or her integrity ("a high influence value", Maxwell, 1993: 39, "a solid reputation"; Maxwell, 1993: 41) and credibility; and as a leader, one's integrity builds the people's trust of one (Maxwell, 1993: 38). Note that a leader must truly be a man of high integrity (Owen, 2012). It is better to live truth instead of expressing or voicing it and one stands tall. Smartly, (s)he should thus maintain the trust of others while up-keeping relationships with the people and others.

Of significance, Gagliardi (2011; in **bold**, authors' emphasis) highlighted that the most common misreading among people who have not studied Sun Tzu's work (**or even most Chinese war strategies**) is that its basic competitive philosophy is Machiavellian, empty of ethical considerations in advancing its principles of success in competitive arenas. Nothing could be further from the truth. On the contrary, Sun Tzu imparts that ethical behavior is the foundation for success in competition.

Horsager (2012) presented another precious pointer; he underscored that, "people notice those who do what is right ahead of what is easy. Leaders who have built this pillar consistently do what needs to be done when it needs to be done, whether they feel like doing it or not. It is the work of life to do what is right rather than what is easy". And interestingly too, this is echoed in Krause (1997: 40) who stressed that leaders "seek what is right rather than to accept what is easy; to show courage and patience in times of crisis".

Krause (1997: 98) also pertinently pinpointed these, "wealth and power by forfeiting the principles underlying your character cannot possibly bring you contentment" or even peace of mind.

8 The Commander Should Be Wise; Wisdom Is Better than Mere Knowledge or Having Certain Information

Chin-Ning Chu once pointed out that, "Before you journey, (be wise,) observe the wind carefully, detect its direction, and then follow it. You will get to your destination twice as fast with half the effort." (afterQuotes, 2014, cited in Low and Teo, 2014).

Of significance, having wisdom is better than having mere knowledge or having certain information. Being wise is to "having the power of discerning and judging properly as to what is true or right; possessing discernment, judgment, or discretion"; it is also "characterised by or showing such power; judicious or prudent: a wise decision" (Dictionary.com, 2014, cited in Low and Teo, 2014).

Sun Tzu's *The Art of War* can also be seen as teaching us to stop defining successful in terms of winning conflicts or in terms of beating opponents (Gagliardi, 2011). To elaborate, there is wisdom, and that wisdom is about or in having peaceful cooperation, collaboration, creation of alliances, teamwork, win-win, enjoyment of mutual benefits and synergies, and they are better than having friction or conflicts and waging war and competing. Take, for example, the creation of an economic union such as the European Union (EU) can lead to mutual benefits and increasing economic efficiency as well as establishing closer political and cultural ties between the member countries.

As a good gardener prepares the soil, so a wise leader creates and cultivates a setting that promotes community (Dreher, 1996). Tao in fact urges us to look for the underlying harmony beyond apparent division and accord – and one by suspending judgment and practicing patience and presence to affirm the Taoist principle of Oneness (Dreher, 1996: 186). Conflict is neither good nor bad, but it is how one responds to it. And interestingly, in Japan, the word for community is "wa" or harmony, and leadership has always meant responsibility for maintaining "wa"; conflicts are opportunities to learn, "transforming competition into cooperation (and) creating heaven from its opposite". (Dreher, 1996: 119).

Indeed the best war is never fought. It is better to "win without fighting" (Sun Tzu, cited in Michaelson, 2001: 22). Strategies are preferred to the use of force or violence; Sun Tzu said that "complete victory is when the army does not fight" (Cleary 1991; also cited in Low, 2010a: 99). This is tantamount to Lao Tzu's using light to return to Light. Then one can breathe one's last breath yet be ever living.

Low (2010a) also highlighted that although ancient China often had many wars and internal strife, the wise Chinese general tried very hard to avoid wars and violence. The "Big Peace" is subscribed to. Ordinarily, non-violence was embraced, and war or violence was and is seen or deemed necessary as the last resort. To win without fighting is better than winning with losses. According to Sun Tzu, in war, the winning strategist only seeks battle after success has been secured or gained, where as those who is fated to defeat first fights and afterwards looks for victory.

True one may also argue that Sun Tzu's ethics are pragmatic rather than idealistic. He focuses on the fact that direct conflict is innately costly (Gagliardi, 2011). Those who naturally react to competitive situations by wanting to engage in battles and defeat their opponents are ruined to defeat, even if they time and again win their battles. However, this is also real in marketing warfare as it is in military fights; Sun Tzu advances the art of war as a strategy for swopping the artless, destructive conflicts that define most competitive battles, including those that too often occur among business rivals. Sun Tzu's analysis is that victorious conflict is so naturally costly that it is never worthy or meaningful. A business can win a market by spending too much money, but it cannot make a profit doing so.

9 The Commander Should Run Away – and to Return to Fight Again

A killed or dead hero is not good or beneficial. As such, another useful strategy is to run away – especially when one knows that one is losing the battle or the war. And this is often a good option. For (s)he who survives or lives for another day can return to fight again.

In the modern-day context, companies can do research and development to innovate and improve their products or train and grow their people to be better skilled and equipped (Michaelson, 2001). They "develop what is good in others, minimise what is bad... Promote people who have talent; train those who lack skill." (Krause, 1997: 99). Strategic leaders can also "find the best leaders and copy their methods. In this way, you will also discover the meaning of leadership." (Krause, 1997: 35). They can also recruit professionals and quality people to build up their organisation, on its wings or strengthening itself to counter and manoeuvre any competitive actions made by their opponents.

10 The Commander Should Go into Uncontested Area(s) [The Commander's and the People's Overall Success and Victory is Non-Warfare]

To advance the point made earlier, most wars are not necessary, and the best wars are not often fought. Winning without fighting is always the best option. If there is no fighting or violence, all parties or everyone wins. Fighting, warfare and violence involves deaths, losses and a waste of resources. Having said these, then again, amidst chaos... or to apply Sun Tzu's words (cited in Goodreads, 2014, cited in Low and Teo, 2014), "In the midst of chaos, there is also opportunity". Perhaps, the leader needs to capitalise the situation, assembling and marshalling the conditions, being smart to change the playing field while seizing the prevailing chances.

It is worthy to note that Sun Tzu also teaches that all of us depend on others to create opportunities for ourselves. Every marketplace has unfulfilled needs, just as every business has weaknesses. Both are opportunities for improving our position, and frequently those opportunities are masked as problems. All of us do not recognize these opportunities simply because we are not trained to see them in the challenges that face us (Gagliardi, 2011).

All of us must move. Leaders must move. It's about in search of excellence and not perfection (Dreher, 1996). And to paraphrase Gary Comer (cited in Pencak, 2014), when a leader worries about being better; bigger will take care of itself.

Strategic leaders keep on climbing mountains. Learning is an essential part of our nature (Niven, 2000; Dreher, 1996; Krause, 1997). They "seek understanding like a thirsty man lost in the dessert seeks water – with fearful determination" (Krause, 1997: 70; Niven, 2000). Strategic leaders never stop learning and adapting (Niven, 2000), and they (Tao leaders) "realise their unlimited capacity for growth" (Dreher, 1996: 75). The strategic leader's art of advantage and maximising opportunity here lies in learning, adopting and adapting a blue ocean strategy. In business and marketing, the leader should lead the people into the blue ocean, uncontested or unrivalled grounds (for example, growing markets; strategic moves simply create a leap in value for the company, its buyers, and its employees, while unlocking new demand and making the competition irrelevant; Kim and Mauborgne, 2005, cited in Low and Teo, 2014) as opposed to the red ocean which is competitive, and a saturated, price-cutting or discount-giving marketplace, that is, indeed crowded with many players.

As a prelude to the conclusion, perhaps it is good to see the key points as listed in *Figure 1*; it shows the 10 key lessons of strategic leadership thinking garnered from the various Chinese War Strategies.

Figure 1: shows the 10 key strategic leadership thinking and insights gleaned from the various Chinese War Strategies.

Conclusion

Leaders must be able to coax, persuade, encourage, influence and sway their people (Maxwell, 1993; Low, 2013a). And strategic leaders are thus wise, effectively persuasive, motivating, even inspiring and influential.

Besides, strategic leaders keep on ascending, climbing mountains, learning, venturing and conquering new territories. And they are able to convince and get their people and others to follow them. As Winston Churchill wisely said (Woopidoo! 2014), "However beautiful the strategy, you should occasionally look at the results", leaders should ultimately get their people to attain and achieve! Strategic leaders indeed get results, outcomes and accomplishments.

Chapter 5

Forward Thinking & Planning

"The best way to predict the future is to create it."
Peter Drucker

A blind musician used to carry a lantern whenever he was out in the night. One day, a man asked him, "Why are you carrying the lantern? It serves no purpose for you!" "It's to prevent people from bumping or knocking into me," replied the blind man.

What Is A Plan?

Plan is a method worked out or formulated beforehand for achieving a desired result. Simply put, one cannot reap (get results or rewards) without sowing (planning). My experience as a *kampung boy* has taught me that planning is like a china egg. If you have ever kept chickens, you will know that a china egg will at times encourage them to lay real eggs.

What Is Planning?

Planning is the process of setting specific goals and courses of actions, prior to taking action. Planning should indeed be part of our habits, both at personal and professional levels.

Planning is a must for business success. Fail to plan and you plan to fail.

Planning is usually difficult since there is no immediate feedback as to its value. However, if you think of running yourself (your business) in the same way you might think about climbing a mountain, the purpose and benefits of planning become even clearer.

When you start up the mountain you never know what to expect. Anything can happen – a sudden change in weather, lost or broken equipment, an injury, mistakes in maps. Planning for these eventualities will allow you to deal with them and still reach your objective in spite of temporary setbacks. On the contrary, lack of planning can spell disaster. The more careful the planning, the more likely problems will be anticipated and not allowed to interfere with your ultimate business objective.

We need to plan for contingencies too. A contingency is something that might occur but again, it might not. If it does occur, it will generally be least expected. Examples of contingencies include a flat tyre, an unexpected guest or a stock market crash are. Contingencies can indeed immobilise us. Contingency plans, just simple ones, as having a spare tyre in your car qualifies. Such plans enhance your awareness of possible problems and you adopt the Boy Scouts' motto: "Be prepared".

Planning is Time Consuming?

However, people may find and fault planning as being time-consuming; "they got better things to do". Or that "we should live for today, and <u>not</u> for tomorrow." But why not take a minute and think about planning to avoid contingencies? Then again, sometimes due to stubbornness, most people don't plan. They leave it to chances. They are swimming upstream! What they should be aware is that no one relying on chance alone has ever been consistently successful. Success does not happen by luck or chance alone. It comes from hard work, planning and preparation.

In fact, the key to improving your luck and reducing your risks is planning! Planning will help you upkeep a high level of readiness, come high waters or hailstorms! You will recognise good fortune when it appears, and then take advantage of the opportunity it presents. And with that, you will also experience a tremendous surge of fulfilment and confidence that will linger with you for a long time to come.

Thinking Always Ahead

> *"Strive with diligence, and be a lamp unto yourselves."*
> *Buddha*

"Strive to accomplish your ambitions and gain the summit of your abilities... ...Above all, never give up" (Christopher Lee, *actor*).

And "thinking always ahead, thinking always of trying to do more, brings a state of mind in which nothing seems impossible." These words from Henry Ford remind us that we need to plan and think about our future, taking a long-term view of things.

The Benefits of Forward Thinking and Planning

According to Peter Drucker, planning is action taken today to reach tomorrow's goals. We decide what we need to do today to prepare ourselves or the organisation for an uncertain future.

Thoughtful and forward planning have led to many companies' great financial results. Many great companies have also found that planning increases incomes or market share or both. And some find planning as the way to save their ailing businesses.

Organisational strengths can also be born out of forward thinking and planning. And managers grow and develop themselves when they quickly learn and think strategically.

Overall, planning has its advantages and benefits. Planning:

O Planning clarifies; it helps one to work out clearly what one really wants out of life by cutting through all the superfluities that clutter one's mind.

O Provides direction and it gives a sense of purpose for oneself (and the company).

O Prepares us for contingencies.

O Stimulates us to think about the promise of the future.

O Reduces compartmentalised, separated or piecemeal decision-making that is inconsistent with the company's overall direction. A plan provides a unifying framework against which decisions can be assessed.

O Reveals future opportunities and threats. According to Peter Drucker, planning can help identify potential opportunities and threats and at least minimise long-term risks.

O Provides standards, planning helps size up your performance, measure progress, and work out how well you are doing.

O Enables control, ensuring activities conform to plans, in which standards are set, performance measured against; these standards and deviations (if any) are identified and then rectified.

O Explores, generates and stimulates new ideas; indeed, good planners look for new ideas, or new strategies and growth.

Leaders Have Visions

When we plan, we need to have visions.

Vision refers to the category of intentions that are broad, all-inclusive and forward thinking. It is, in fact, an aspiration for the future; there is this hope. Planning is strongly associated with visioning. And corporate leaders need to present very clear directions for the company's future. They need to identify priorities, opportunities and vulnerabilities.

Leaders must work, i.e., visioning and planning and workers must lead which means that doers should be planners and plan their work. People want to be involved in creating what they have to execute. This is good since with the right guidance, they do better (involved and working on the specific details) than what the leaders do.

We should not lose sight of our vision. To lose sight of our vision is similar to, as the story goes…

Once there lived a Persian prince who married a beautiful princess. They lived a life of perfect bliss for a year before she then died. The prince mourned grievously and had her body placed in a silver casket.

A short time later, he put the casket in a small garden. Not long later, he beautified the garden, and a small pond was added to enhance the setting. Still later, several trees and flowering plants were added, and so on. After two years has passed, one day, he sat gazing at several acres of lakes with swans, elaborate flower beds and elegant tree arrangements and he noticed in the centre of it all lay the silver casket.

After contemplating for some time, he pointed out at the casket and ordered his men to remove it, saying, "It's an eye sore! It is one thing that is spoiling the beautiful garden."

The message of the story is obvious and unfortunately, it happens to organisations; bureaucracy sets in. There are endless procedures, meaningless rules and methods that have lost their original meaning and place in helping us to achieve our vision and goals. The original ideas, usually clear and unpretentious, become so enmeshed in endless procedures and organised "splendour" (impressive, voluminous procedure manuals) that the true spirit of the company's or founder's vision is lost.

Do not over rely on methods.

If **how** it's done becomes more important than **whether** it's done, then methods and procedures will gradually take over the entire goal-setting process; and sadly though, your dreams for the future will evaporate.

Be aware of other dangers in planning. No matter good you think your plans are when you first start out, you still have to allow for modification and improvement along the way as new concept germinates and begins to bear fruits.

"One does <u>not</u> plan and then try to make the circumstances fit those plans. One tries to make plans fit the circumstances."

General G. Patton

Feeling Afraid?

It appears that the arrival of foreign talents and MNCs (multinational corporations) often looks like a death sentence to our local companies and employees alike. But can these really be threats? You may ask "How can we compete with these Goliaths, they who have much financial and technological resources, their seasoned management, and their powerful international brands?"

Is there any basis to worry about? Not if we use our brains like sushi knife – that is, with forward thinking and planning.

Facing Adversity

It is very easy to be negative, thinking of all the various impossibilities. Local employees and in fact, companies indeed often have more solutions than they might think. These solutions vary, depending on the strength of globalisation pressures in an industry and the nature of an individual or a company's competitive assets.

Size Does Not Matter!

What matters most is quality, rather than bigger or more! A quality-advantage is certainly beneficial, so powerful that fellow rivals would find little chance to defeat you in the marketplace – and this can be an article of faith! Companies can then differentiate themselves, becoming lions in the global marketplace through quality.

Being small is not necessarily bad. Remember small boats, rather than big ships, can be and are quick to respond and move quickly.

And like David, we need to think laterally. Don't assume boundaries that are not there. A stag with a pair of beautiful antlers became entangled in some bushes and she had, all this while, been thinking un-lovingly about her legs. But when the hunters came, she jerked, her antlers became untangled, bounded away to safety and the legs that she disliked so much saved her.

The Value of Globalisation

Regionalisation and globalisation are strategic ways in which a business can survive the frequent and unexpected changes in the economy, like the recent Asian currency meltdown.

Should the globalisation pressures become strong (no one can escape from this, it is evident!) and with the resources, it can always seek strategic alliances or partnerships abroad. If a company has no competitive assets that it can transfer to other countries, it can also retreat to a locally oriented link within the value chain. But if globalisation pressures are weak, the company can defend its market share by leveraging the advantages it enjoys in its home market such as better knowing the locals' tastes, consumer behaviours, dislikes and preferences. The Company knows the market best!

By the same token, Singaporean employees know Singapore best – their individual strengths.

Or you could be that person who is convinced that all cultures are equally good, and besides, you like and enjoy learning the rich variety of foreign cultures. Then, you as an employee may decide to venture abroad, find out if there is a posting abroad; add some spice, try your life as an expat! Be an ambassador! Be like the crane that replies to the peacock which criticises her for the dullness of her plumage. "I'm not denying that my feathers are much duller than yours, but when it comes to flying I can soar into clouds, whereas you are confined to the earth like any dunghill cock."

Going global, many companies in emerging markets have the strengths that can work well in other countries. Singapore companies can work well in Greater China or any country in the Asian region. And those that operate in industries where the globalisation pressures are weak may well able to extend their success to several other markets that are similar to their home base. Those operating in global markets may be able to contend head-on with multinational rivals. Employees in such companies need to improve their language(s), etiquette and multicultural skills.

"As the world changes, you've got to reposition yourself against the future" (Ries, Al and Trout, Jack, 1997: 185).

Valuing New Knowledge

> *"We will have to evolve a comprehensive national lifelong learning system that continually retrains our workforce, and encourages every individual to learn all the time as a matter of necessity. We must have thinking workers and a learning workforce. In fact the whole country must become a learning nation."*
>
> *– PM Goh Chok Tong, May Day Rally 1998*

Knowledge is power! Singapore workers must indeed make themselves obsolete before others or someone else does. So we need to reposition ourselves! Niche ourselves in the new knowledge and its applications.

Through learning the company ways and by better understanding the relationship between the individual's/ their company's strengths or assets and the industry they operate in, executives and employees alike can gain a clearer picture of the solution(s) they really have when foreign talents/ multinationals come to stay in Singapore.

Indeed, with stronger competition we galvanise and build ourselves, emerging stronger. We feed ourselves with knowledge and technologies as if they were manna from heaven!

Knowledge's principal goal is to create men who are capable of doing new things. Knowledge is indeed related to growth and technological advances can be its contributing factor. With people as wealth, innovation and long-term growth does not have to come from some external mystery source but created as returns to investment (like better use of machines, organising productions, better process knowledge and applications) within the economic system. Knowledge spread freely and multiplies. Human capital investments thus raise productivity and increase the quality of our workforce.

Singapore companies can be forward-looking, capitalising on knowledge while taking stock of ideas, benchmarking and networking as well as stressing on people – humanistic values – and quality values so as to nurture a culture that is conducive to idea-generation and innovation-diffusion. "Inch by inch, it becomes a cinch."

Here, economist Paul Romer gives a good analogy, swimming. Every year there are improvements in the swimming records, marked improvements. The swimmer can push him(her)self through physical training. However, a breakthrough – the crawl stroke more effective than breast stroke – was discovered and the new knowledge being applied. And of course, later, much pool-time is saved with the continuous refinements or growth in the overall swimming techniques. Further examples are the advances in scientific and non-scientific knowledge with its uses in creating new products and new markets such as the use – through satellite technology – of flat-panel televisions and portable phones anywhere in the world.

Valuing Partnerships

Asians or Chinese, in particular, value *quanxi* or relationships. And put this into an IT jargon, we are living in this world of connectivities. We need to get close, and create opportunities, to be in the same room with our customers and suppliers alike. And networking we must! Learn what they think and what they believe. Find out their needs. Partnering customers and suppliers behave as if they were one company.

The Asian or bamboo network must be tapped if we are thinking strategically. The underlying premise is 'for me to succeed, you must succeed too!' However, we do need right people (key decision-makers), the right partner (who are willing to shift paradigms and drive change) and the right process(es) (that provides maximum benefits to the customers, thereby enhancing the company the competitive edge).

Thus, in whatever we do, we need to have the thinking and confidence to distance ourselves from frustration and objectively say:

> It took about 15 minutes for me to avoid negative labelling. That's too long! I need to re-think and hold my positive values. This is and itself a more concrete and effective strategy – forward thinking and planning – for my personal success.

> Success breeds success!

Your Notes, Ideas
& Action Points

Chapter 6

Strategic Thinking & Organisational Effectiveness

"The ultimate goal of the corporation is survival."
Peter Drucker

"It will make for clearer thinking if we reserve the term 'strategy' for actions aimed directly at altering the strength of the enterprise relative to that of its competitors"
Kenichi Ohmae

"It (strategy) deals with the most fundamental and basic questions that involve the very existence of the whole organisation and guide the whole company's future" (Kerry Napuk). The corporate leader's concerns are not with the day-to-day competition (the operating managers are there to take care of that) but rather with the ways of gaining positions of sustained advantage for the organisations. Loading the odds in the operating managers' favour before the competition takes place, the corporate leader give them superior positions so much so that the competitors believe that the company's position is so strong. Better still, when they concede without a fight.

Loading the odds in the company's favour and putting it into positions of advantage include being of superior efficiency, low costs and/ or differentiation. The company can also include providing quality products and services just like McDonald's with Quality and Mercedes-Benz with status. The key here is for the company and its corporate leaders to identify the distinctive capabilities that appeal to the company's targeted market segment, relative to its competitors. "A company can outperform rivals only if it can establish a difference that it can preserve" (Michael Porter, 1996). If the company can do this, strategic success or positions of strength and higher returns will follow. Or as C. K. Prahalad puts it, "Competing for the future means maintaining continuity by constantly creating new sources of profit."

Simple is Beautiful

Businesses can be simplified and almost every business can have its value raised dramatically by clever simplification. Companies can put themselves into positions of advantage by being simple. Complex is ugly. Simple is beautiful. Simple to express; simple to understand. If strategy is not clear and simple, it is not likely to be effective. And "powerful ideas are (in fact) usually utterly simple: 'safety' for Volvo, 'Overnight' for Federal Express" (Al Ries). And even, McDonald's fast-service, family-friendly fast food. They are all turned into powerful brands by their simple positioning. There is also greater awareness among the company's people and customers as well as clarity about the company and its products and services. People remember them better.

Corporate and Personal Goals

All of us want and seek to accomplish our personal goals. And our personal goals need to be synthesised, or at least identified, with our company goals. The company's leadership must make its vision known to the people. Once its people know the company's vision and goals, the company leaders provide opportunities for the people to participate meaningfully in meeting these company objectives ("Objectives… are direction. …They are not commands, they are commitments." – Peter Drucker). Also, in a way that gives the people a chance for identifying their personal goals. They are motivated to work and in working towards getting the results, they will achieve the company goals and their personal goals. Matched company goals and the individual worker's personal goals mean greater staff satisfaction. In other words, P. A. T. S. is achieved; that is, it leads to higher **P**roductivity, lower **A**bsenteeism, lower **T**urnover (higher staff retention) as well as higher **S**atisfaction among the staff.

Organisational Effectiveness

Organisational effectiveness can also be measured through the attainment of the company's goals. The proponents of effectiveness as meeting or surpassing the organisational goals include Chester Barnard, one of the earliest management theorists. According to Barnard (1938), "when a specified desired end is attained we shall say that the action is 'effective'". The goal approach to effectiveness consists of identifying an organisation's output goals and assessing how well the organisation has attained those goals (Price, 1972: 3 - 15).

Accordingly, if the goal is a 12 percent return on sales, then the furniture division of a particular company (with an average 25 percent annual) is highly effective. If it is 15 new products every year, then a high-tech 'start-up' with more than 60 new product offerings each year, is clearly effective.

It is more productive to measure operative goals (than official goals) as they are more specific. (Official goals are general aims, tend to be abstract and difficult to measure such as a mission statement. Take a community police's mission, for example, one of "giving peace to our neighbourhood" and another of "creating the community's awareness of organised crimes" may be less specific; they are too broad, and rather abstract.) Operative goals represent actual goals, typically pertain to the primary tasks an organisation must perform. And these goals are concerned with the key result areas (KRAs) i.e., overall performance, profitability, productivity (to produce more goods and services with less inputs), innovation (innovate or evaporate!), market share (e.g. achieving total sales of 100,000 units a year by Year 20____), management performance (good management), employee training and development and social responsibility. Peter F. Drucker indicates the 8 key result areas (KRAs) as (1) market share (2) innovation (3) productivity (4) physical and financial resources (5) profitability (6) manager performance and development (7) employee performance and attitude, and (8) social responsibility. Drucker contends that an organisation must establish goals in each area vital to its existence. Though principally applicable to profit-oriented companies, Drucker's eight (8) KRAs are also relevant for public sector and other not-for-profit ventures. (Please see Drucker, Peter F. (1954) <u>The Practice of Management</u>, New York, Harper and Row, p. 62 - 87).

In a not-for-profit organisation, say, a community's Police Force, the organisation can be assessed in terms of its goal attainment. Let me illustrate. One of its operative goals, say under innovation, can be the Police Force's introduction of at least three (3) new products or services per year (such as a new management information system (M.I.S.), bicycle patrols, park watch groups) for the community it looks after. Or the Police can acquire or invest in at least one sophisticated equipment or technological innovation, each year to better assist in its criminal investigations. The drop in crime rates, the number of triads smashed and hardcore cases solved would help assess the achievement of such goals. Under employee performance, the goals can be evaluated in terms of the number of senior and junior police officers trained in the respective Senior and Junior Command courses, locally and/ or overseas attachments. And the Police Force can also encourage its men to learn new skills such as IT skills and the numbers trained collated. Under social responsibility, the Police may decide to hold at least 3 exhibitions and school talks each year to raise the community or public awareness of organised crimes.

For a profit organisation like a manufacturing concern, examples of its operative goals can include (1) increasing its productivity (production of its goods) by 10 percent and (2) reducing its production costs by 5 percent. Under its operative goal of increasing productivity, the evaluative criteria can be in ensuring the training of its workers, all its workers will have to go through the Critical Enabling Skills (Crest Training) and OJT (On-the-job Training). And this goal will also be evaluated in terms of the introduction or use of at least 1 equipment or technological innovation during the period under review. As for its operative goal of reducing the production costs by 5 percent, this goal would be achieved by the firm's use of cheaper foreign labour, outsourcing of its human resources function and bulk-buying or buying in cash to get lower prices and/or discounts for the company's supplies.

The use of goal approach is favoured particularly so in business organisations where output goals can be readily measured. Business firms typically evaluate performance in terms of profitability (net profits), growth (increase in total assets, sales, etc.), market leadership (market leadership), stockholder wealth (dividends plus stock appreciation), use of resources (return on investment: ROI) and contributions to employees (employment security, salaries and wages).

Ensuring the Organisation's Long Term Survival

In any case, organisations need to pursue a variety or multiplicity of goals to ensure long-term survival. Some of these goals, however, can be potentially conflicting e.g. decreasing price can normally increase market share though price decrease may lower the company's profits.

Since the goal approach represents the interests of the managers and usually that of the company owners, we can perhaps marry the goal approach to the stakeholder or multiple-constituency approach, highlighting the organisation's relationship with and the importance of the larger environment. Goals can also be applied to a workout list of the organisation's various stakeholders in which case, this approach attempts to satisfy a wide range of diverse and multiple stakeholders, not just the company owners. Zooming out and looking beyond the company would enable us to think outside the box.

Stakeholders are the individuals and groups who influence and are influenced by how well the organisations are managed. They usually include the organisation itself, stockowners and investors, government, suppliers, customers, employees and society at large. Meeting the interests of the various stakeholders is fast becoming the 21st. Century's realities and demands for many organisations. Corporate leaders normally engage in a balancing act. They try to minimally satisfy diverse preferences for performance to ensure a continued supply of scarce and needed resources from various stakeholders.

Additionally, we can also apply McKinsey's 7S Framework to evaluate a company's organisational effectiveness, which is, assessing whether the organisation's goals have been attained in terms of each of these dimensions:

Staff: How well is the company able to recruit, select, retain high-calibre staff?

Structure: How is the company organised?

Systems: How well is the company coping or adapting with information technology (IT)/ technology?

Style: What is the company's management style? Is it of theory X or that of Theory Y? How well do the style motivate or inspire the staff?

Shared values: What are the company's shared beliefs? Do any if these values help the company to attain its goals?

Skills: How competent are the company's people? Are the people well-trained?

Strategy: How well are the company's goals achieved?

The 7S Framework helps us to focus our attention on many issues, both internal and external that will affect the company's effectiveness.

The Benefits of Organisational Goals

Nonetheless, viewed from the big picture perspective, goals provide several important benefits. These benefits are that goals:

O Serve as guidelines for action or "what should be done". They provide the staff the focus on what to do, directing their efforts and energies. Goals help the company to be on track, moving forward and achieving. After all, conversely, as Seneca (4 B.C. – A.D. 65) once said, "our plans miscarry because they have no aim (goal). When a man does not know what harbour he is making for, no winds is the right wind."

O Prescribe on what "should not be".

O Give a source of legitimacy, justifying the company's activities and its very existence to such stakeholder groups such as customers, employees, owners and the society. Legitimacy is that belief that 'the organisation is good' or that 'the organisation has the necessary goodness to continue its operations'. For example, take the case of a hospital that has been helping the community in curing sick people and preventing diseases. Indeed, an organisation whose goals are deemed legitimate enjoys a greatly enhanced ability to get resources and support from the environment.

O Offer standards of performance. Since the goals are clearly stated, they offer direct standards for assessing an organisation's performance. Once an organisation establishes goals in quantifiable areas such as sales, profits, the degree to which they have achieved should be easily verifiable.

O Serve as vital source of motivation for the staff. They pose a challenge; they tell what characterise success and prescribe on how to achieve it. Organisational goals are often incentives for the company people. Take an example of a bank. One of the bank branch's goals is to increase sales of unit trusts and investment products. It pursues this goal with a wide-ranging incentive programme. Every bank officer who tops $1,000,000 in fortnightly sales, gets a special 10 grams gold wafer. Other incentive awards for accomplishing different goals include cash awards, gift vouchers and vacation trips.

O   Provide the rationale for organising. Organisational goals provide a basis for organisational design. In order, for example, to encourage more innovation within the organisation, people are organised, working in teams (a flatter structure), self-directing and making their own decisions while enjoying co-ownership.

Additionally, learning organisations in a knowledge-based economy can tie-in the individuals' learning to their companies' business goals. The learning contract should specify the knowledge and skills that the employee should acquire over the next year to meet the individual goals. These individual employee's goals are then tied directly to the departmental and business unit goals; and should have a direct relation to the company's overall business goals. In this way, it not only makes each employee accountable and performing, but also every employee learns, fulfilling both the employee's and the company's needs.

Theoretically speaking, because the learning contract is directly tied to business goals, any learning activity undertaken should lead to a positive change in business results.

On Strategies

We need to remember that 'what got you here won't keep you here!' Things change, the world changes fast enough to invalidate much of what your company is doing today. So where do you want to go from here?

A strategy is, basically, what are you going to do to get there, that is, where you want to go. It is a plan for interacting with the competitive environment to attain the company's goals.

One or a combination of Porter's generic strategies may then be applied. And these include firstly, by focusing, that is, by concentrating on specific or particular market segments. Companies can focus, specialise and create a niche for themselves in particular market segment(s). Here, they can adopt the 'big fish in a small pond' strategy; it is better to occupy the top rung of a smaller ladder than the bottom rung of a larger ladder. A cloth company may specialise in producing clothes for very tall or huge people. And a law firm can choose to specialise in litigation and bankruptcy cases only.

Secondly, by differentiating, that is by distinguishing the products and services or the company itself *in the eyes of the customers* from others in the industry. The company can, for instance, create very recognisable brand names. It can provide the best distribution of its products/ services; and it can be on the leading edge in new product features. In fact, its uniqueness can take many forms. And they offer to their customers what their rivals don't have or cannot offer.

A maverick, by definition, is a new entrant that adopts a strategy radically different from that of existing rivals in the market. And the best hope for an existing company to become a maverick is to embrace change or perhaps even appoint a maverick-type individual as its CEO.

According to McMillan, Ian and R. G. McGrath, R. G. (1997: 3), "a company (in fact) has the opportunity to differentiate itself at every point where it comes in contact with its customers – from the moment customers realise that they need a product or service to the time they no longer want it and decide to dispose of it. For example, "can you make the buying process more convenient and less irritating? Look for the ideal situation, in which competitors' procedures actually discourage people from selecting their products, while your procedures encourage people to come to you. Citibank for example for years captured a significant share of the college student market for credit cards simply by making it easy for students to obtain a card while competitors made it difficult" (McMillan, Ian and R. G. McGrath, R. G. 1997: 5).

Thirdly, through low-cost leadership, by creating a market share advantage over the competitors through low-cost production, greater efficiency and cost-reductions (very tight cost control). Some companies achieve low-cost position through economies of scale and by their position in the experience curve. Others cut their costs through industrial engineering approaches or by effective purchasing of their materials and supplies.

Other strategies involve companies improving the quality of its products and services, embarking on an ever-continuous improvement process. Building on existing organisational capabilities, the company can also stress on innovations, especially new product innovations. The company further invests in staff training and R & D (research and development). When a business keeps on improving itself, it becomes a moving target. Its rivals may find it harder to hit it.

Companies can also increase its profits through a number of strategic ways. They can, for example, increase their profits by better asset turns or planned downsizing – getting smaller to be more profitable.

Perhaps, the best strategy could be the simplest strategy. What I have in mind is what lies behind Konosuke Matsushita's saying, that is, "when it rains, put up your umbrella". Simply put, we should follow the obvious, natural order of things in every aspect of life. In business, companies need only to make good products, sell them for a fair profit and be sure to get paid for the business to succeed.

Here, Matsushita constantly consider how best to abide by the laws of nature, how best to "do the right thing" and to continually seek out new definitions of new concepts. It is critical to rely on and apply what Matsushita terms as the "*sunao mind*", translated in English as the "untrapped mind". "An untrapped mind is one that is not biased, that can see things as they truly are. (The untrapped mind sees many possibilities, humble enough to learn from anyone and anything and is perceptive enough to see things as they are.) This is why Matsushita worked untiringly to achieve his life's goal of the "untrapped mind". (*Source: Konosuke Matsushita 1894- 1989 his Life & His Legacy* in <u>Asia 21</u>, January 2000, PHP, p. 38 – 43).

Overall, much of the success of any strategy depends on how creative the thinking is that leads to that strategy. Rigid, within-the-box, traditional strategic thinking often spawns narrow strategies. Break out of the box. "Success in the past has no implication for success in the future... The formulas for yesterday's success are almost guaranteed to be formulas for failure tomorrow", asserts Michael Hammer. C K Prahalad, on the other hand, speaks of "escap(ing) the gravitational pull of the past... (by being) willing to challenge... (our) own orthodoxies."

Recreating the Company

Indeed, as Warren Bennis urges, twenty-first century leaders need to make sure that they are constantly reinventing the organisations. Leaders must cleverly deploy their people's creativity to recreate the company.

And to these, the researcher - writers would add that organisations must avoid 'groupthink' (Janis) if they are to better their strategic thinking and planning. Over-cohesive teams (such as planning teams) can lose their capacity for critical evaluations, and Janis called this 'groupthink'. Several characteristics of a group's behaviours show that 'groupthink' may be occurring when the group:

O Believes it is beyond criticism that it should not and cannot be criticised.

O Refuses to accept unpleasant or contradictory data.

O Believes the group is above criticism from outsiders (e.g. suppliers or society-at-large stakeholders), protecting itself from 'disturbing' ideas from outside.

O Refuses to tolerate members who suggest it may be wrong.

O Sees opposition as weak, evil or stupid.

O Assumes consensus exists without checking with members.

Indeed, 'groupthink' can result in poor, ill-considered decisions because of inaccurate information, failure to consider alternatives and failure to examine risks. To me, 'groupthink' is akin to within-the-box thinking!

To avoid the negative consequences of 'groupthink', group members are encouraged to assess ideas and courses of actions. And here are some suggested ways to avoid or minimise 'groupthink'; they include:

O Recruiting independent or even foreign talent directors and managers to the Company.

O Getting advice from and discuss issues with outside consultants and experts.

O Getting feedback from the staff or customers regarding issues affecting them.

O Being receptive to outside criticisms (e.g. feedback from a third party or outsiders, general surveys done with staff and customers, etc.).

O When getting input, team leader(s) should avoid taking position during the discussion(s). Groups should be working together towards consensus instead of adopting the stance of the dominating leader(s).

O Creating sub-groups, have a contingent "what-if" plan and appoint a critical evaluator.

O Being open-minded (remember that our mind is like a parachute. For it to work, it has to be open), thinking broadly & globally.

O Letting a team member play the devil's advocate at each meeting.

O Top management working towards being receptive to outside criticisms such as that coming from staff, and customers.

O Subjecting the decision to a vote or having an open discussion to see or consider other viewpoints when a decision is to be made.

O Having group rotation to increase cohesiveness within department (e.g. every 3 months once).

O Having group evaluation (measure the desired outcome against actual performance).

O Members having confidence, are also given assurance that they would not be punished when they disagree with the ideas/opinions or suggestions of the dominating team members or leaders.

We must move out of our comfort zone, make paradigm shift and use wider boundaries when we think, plan and evaluate/ continuously improve. We should practise free-form strategic thinking, coming out with not-tried-before strategies while playing to our competitors' weaknesses.

Scanning the Environment

Scan the environment (outside the organisation). We need to do an OUTSIDE-IN thinking; that is more PRO-ACTIVE. Bending our sail to factor in the winds, taking advantage of them. We should do an outside-in rather than an inside-out planning. Inside-out planning tends to be more reactive – using this approach may not encourage the organisation, being the centre and making an outside contribution, to ask: "if my organisation is the solution, what's the problem" and thus we may miss any chances or new areas of opportunities.

With an outside-in thinking and planning, there will always be windows of OPPORTUNITIES, they often open and close quickly! Search for these windows. Be open to change. Remember what create opportunities – IT'S CHANGE! Others see the same changes that create discomfort or anxieties for some executives as strategic opportunities. And these opportunities, to name a few, include:

O Change in customer demographics
O Change in quality and customer service expectations/ perceptions
O Entry or exit of firms
O Rivalry among the key players
O Change in the way buyers and sellers communicate
O Change in industry standards and practices
O Change of government/ national administration

O   Release of governmental/ military technology

O   Changes in our sociology e.g. population increases, more working women, etc.

O   Entry or exit of a foreign player.

Your Notes, Ideas
& Action Points

Chapter 7

Strategies: Competitive & Co-operative And Organisational Excellence

"Tap your suppliers' strengths, involve them and create that extended family feeling of your company among your suppliers."

"Think partnering. Think mutual help and long term. Build trust and collaborate."

Patrick Low Kim Cheng

Strategies: Competitive and Co-operative

Companies can take the traditional stance or orientation, which is to compete with others, or adopt a co-operative or partnership stance.

Competitive or Adversarial Strategies

Competitive or adversarial strategies assume that resources are scarce; and therefore organisations must compete for these scarce resources.

Companies attempt to minimise their dependence on other companies for the supply of important resources. Some common forms of resource dependency include accesses to markets, technology, special skills and raw materials. And companies also attempt to influence the environment to make these resources available. When threatened with greater dependence, companies will certainly assert control over external resources to minimise that dependence. And according to this resource dependence theory, no company wants to become or feel vulnerable to other companies as being vulnerable can indeed lead to negative effects on their performance. Proponents of this resource dependency theory include Pfeffer and Salancik (1978).

Here, under the competitive strategies, my discussions will be on both the defender's and prospector's strategies and strategic decisions that a company can adopt.

The Defender

With its usual characteristic **strong technical and market knowledge**, the defender has **a narrow product line and a small market share** in which it operates. Usually, the defender may seek <u>not</u> to expand or seize new market opportunities but its emphasis is on **defending a patch through a narrow target market. The defender's pricing may be aggressive with strong advertising**.

And with a routine technical core and a usually **crisp structure** (here, the organisational structure is usually of an inflexible, mechanistic or bureaucratic nature), the defender focuses on the efficiency of its present technology with cost efficiency production. In fact, the whole logic of this strategy is geared towards maintaining alternatives in the task environment. And the defender organisation has to be **always on the move** as well as being restless.

Here, the defender strategy is particularly **suitable for a stable-open environment** with many buyers and many sellers, and the business is usually in its mature stage.

We should note however that the defender is usually susceptible to **errors of decision under-capacity**. After all, the defender's decision-making tends to be concentrated in the financial or production function.

The Prospector

In this strategy, the organisation is likely to **look for new market opportunities** and staying close to the competition; the prospector's priority is to compete by staying ahead of the rivals.

(Here, an explanation of fuzzy structure is necessary. It means the organisational structure is organic, and is capable of adapting to outside changes. Such organic structures are usually regarded by decision-makers as flexible; and it is the intention rather than the letter of the rule that counts. Rules are not regarded as cast in tablets of stones and are liable to change according to an ill-defined set of circumstances). Consisting normally of **a fuzzy structure**, the prospector is usually in the **experimental mode**. The prospector experiments with new products or services in response to the environmental demands or trends. Here, it usually **uses technology and price efficiency to compete**.

The logic of the prospector's strategy is to **maintain alternatives by ensuring that the organisation has a new flow of products** to capture the attention of new customers. Hence, it **strives on the uncertainties and changes in the markets**.

The prospector's strategy will be **suitable in a task environment** (defined specifically in terms of the company's customers, suppliers, employees and government regulatory agencies) **where there are many buyers and sellers**, but its goal is to try and steal temporary monopoly by creating a protective niche before its competitors follow.

The prospector may, however, suffer inefficiency in its experimentation and is, in a way, susceptible to **errors of decision over-capacity**. Here, the decisions are likely to be made by the R & D or the marketing function.

Overall, companies compete with each other when they believe in the tradition of individualism and self-reliance. Effecting competitive strategies is more like a war, a win-lose situation.

The alternative, co-operate with the competitors. Yes, you've heard it right.

Indeed, it appears that nowadays, no company can go or do it alone when faced with the constant onslaught of increased international competition, changing technology, and new regulations. Indeed, there is growing turbulence of international economic affairs. We see, for example, just to name a few, the ensuing oil crises of 1970's, the subsequent aggravated economic cycles of boom and recession, and the Asian economic meltdown in the late 1990's.

And other major reasons prevail for adopting co-operative strategies; these include companies collaborate, wanting to share:

O   risks when entering new markets, this is particularly so when venturing overseas and entering global markets.
O   cash-in on rewards.
O   (or realise) economies of scale and increase efficiencies.
O   (or realise) speed or action in today's fast moving business world, such as in making for almost instantaneous product launches in the major retail cities.
O   R & D and its costs to bring about costs-savings
O   Greater innovation
O   (or develop) better problem solving ways and increased organisational performance.

In December 1997, for example, Swiss Banking Corporation (SBC) and Union Bank of Switzerland (UBS) merged to be one of the world's largest banks.

From Adversaries to Partners

And "the Way of the sage (or the wise)" as Lao-Tzu (Tao Te Ching) once said, "is to act but not to compete." The world is fast becoming more and more interdependent. More companies are developing inter-organisational co-operative strategies. And partnering is similar to the notion: 'we rather have more friends than make enemies'.

Daft, Richard (1998: 530) speaks of "fresh flowers are blooming on the battle-scarred landscape where once-bitter rivalries among suppliers, customers, and competitors took place. In North America, collaboration among organisations initially occurred in not-for-profit social and mental health organisations to achieve greater effectiveness for each party and better utilise scarce resources."

In 1986, the Chinese Communist government began to allow 100 percent foreign-owned ventures in PRC and the majority of these wholly owned ventures are located in the Special Economic Zones (SEZs). Interestingly, however, only 10 percent of foreign investors have chosen this type of investment. Why? Indeed, they are at a disadvantage when it comes to linking up with the government or government-owned suppliers, service providers and customers (Lassere, Philippe and Schutte, Hellmut (1995: 202). This thus clearly illustrates the importance or benefits of getting (local) partnerships' co-operation and collaboration; having local partners enable access to government officials. (Any Western companies entering into business in China must understand the role of *guanxi* in the Chinese economy. Indeed, *guanxi* is about connections based on relationships and mutual obligations, and that these are often crucial determining criteria for resource allocation decisions.)

Companies can decide which things, if done together with others, would benefit everyone. Once these areas have been decided, companies can then proceed to compete like crazy in other (remaining) areas (the new competition?).

"Nothing is impossible for the man who doesn't have to do it himself" – A. H. Weiler. Companies can get everyone involved and make sure that everyone is involved. And that all are committed or dedicated to hitting the target.

Companies can also partner or involve the customers in defining their goals. Indeed, companies need to bear in mind company goals are useless unless they are based on their customers' needs.

Additionally, companies can tie-up with their suppliers and vendors, particularly those with the knowledge to share about what their companies are doing and/ or the exciting breakthroughs just around the corner. Here, a company collaborates with their suppliers; more so, if these suppliers cannot deliver, then the company cannot achieve its goals. Help your supplier to help you. Think symbiosis, that is, mutual interdependence. When the suppliers' costs decline more than they can achieve alone, the collaborative efforts help improve their productivity. These savings can then be passed on to and help the company.

When partnering, the company can also share its mission and vision statements with its suppliers. Suppliers should know what the company believes and why you believe. Your values and beliefs help define the relationship you/ your company and your supplier(s) develop over time.

The company can also ask to see its suppliers' vision and mission statements. If they don't have any, suggest that they develop one. Also, invite suppliers to the company's celebrations and integrate suppliers to your corporate culture. Let your employees see them in company functions like company's picnics, dinner and dance and other activities. Here, your suppliers will feel like an extended family and they will try harder to satisfy you and your customers.

Also, take your suppliers on a tour of your company's facilities; let them understand your company needs. Suppliers need to understand what happens to their materials, supplies, products and services at your facilities.

Do also ask the suppliers for their ideas, suggestions and inputs. Ask them for their ideas on your company's product or process improvements, do solicit any recommendations which your suppliers have the expertise. In my opinion, suppliers can bring in fresh perspectives that might greatly improve what your company does and how do you do it.

In fact, another reason or key benefit of partnering with your suppliers is that your suppliers can also provide or arrange technical training for your people when your company purchases equipment from them. Besides, they can also provide training on the best ways of using their products and services.

The desirability of collaborative efforts between a company and its suppliers can also be seen in terms of inventory and quality assurance. The just-in-time concept is basically about how to ensure that work in progress moves smoothly through the production process and that any waste (of time, money, materials, etc.) is eliminated or minimised. The company's various suppliers could be linked online to the company. The supplier would then know the company's stock level and supply the necessary raw materials when its inventory runs low. Here, the company buyer's role as tough negotiator is superseded by the role of the supply strategist. A strategic approach to the supply of materials to the company exists; it is proactive and aims at having a precise scheduling of the inflow of goods. Just-in-time management is indeed a vital part of the company's overall approach to quality and customer service.

Companies can have inter-firm alliances in hi-tech areas and these include robotics, IT systems, telecommunications and/or in developing new materials. Joint ventures (JVs), announced co-operative agreements and alliances can be formed. Such alliances are a commonplace, more so, when a single company does not have the knowledge or skills necessary to bring new products to the market. Often, the firms with the knowledge or technology are not even in the same country; such collaborative efforts and partnerships usually involve corporations that headquartered in different nations.

Perhaps, overall, the **5 Cs** framework can be applied to inter-organisational co-operation. The writer will discuss each strategy with its respective possible disadvantages or problems.

1 Control of Other Companies' Stake – Mergers & Acquisitions (M & A)

As a strategic investor, a company can effect strategic purchase(s) of the stake or make investments in other companies to effect co-operation with the latter.

SingTel or Singapore Telecoms International (STI) has taken some stake in Malaysia's Time Engineering. "STI would be offered significant active participation in the management of Time, Time dotCom, Time ISP and their subsidiaries. STI would have at least proportionate representation on the Board of Directors of each of the companies." (The Business Times, 8 Apr 2000, p.1).

Another example include Singapore Airlines (SIA)'s tie-up with Richard Branson's Virgin and SIA also "snaps up 8.3% of Air New Zealand shares" (The Straits Times, 12 Apr 2000, p. 4)

2   Collaborative Networks

Companies network or join together, becoming more cooperative and sharing scarce resources such as that of the STAR Alliance among certain world and regional airlines. In fact, with corporate research budgets under pressure, the recent R & D trends are collaboration.

Many companies are figuring out how to fruitfully connect with outside experts in other firms, consortiums, universities and government bodies. In Singapore, the Singapore Mass Rapid Transit (SMRT) networks with the Nanyang Technological University (NTU). Here, each benefits from the relationship with the other. SMRT would benefit from their possible projects such as: finding new ideas to integrate bus, taxi and rail services, forecasting passenger traffic, developing telecommunication technologies to upgrade the rail network's signaling and communications systems as well as exploring use of materials and how best to upkeep and prevent their damage. NTU, acting as a consultant to SMRT, would also benefit in this new Professorship in Transportation Studies. NTU will be having international experts to lecture at NTU, conduct public seminars and joint research (*SMRT-NTU Tie-up for a Better Transport System*, The Straits Times, 14 January 2000.).

Indeed, through collaborative networks, many big companies are joining forces with smaller firms to get innovative new technologies and markets. Small start-ups or companies then get the larger companies' financing and marketing capabilities.

3   Contracting

Contracts are made when one firm supplies another with specific goods or services at certain times in exchange for a consideration. Here, contracting is a form of boundary management that is most suitable when the organisation initiating the contracts is in a powerful position than the contractee, and when the contract terms are sufficiently tangible to be specified in a written contract.

Some problems could emerge in such a contracting arrangement in that there may be, at times, difficulty to specify certain terms in the contract. For example, the term "good" could imply various levels of excellence. Indeed, it can also be difficult to prepare a written a contract or carry out its terms due to the infinite number of unpredictable possibilities (such as the occurrence of a war or a natural disaster), then the contract will be void. It is sometimes also difficult to enforce the terms of the contract, as in for example, the supplier fails to deliver goods.

4   Coalescing

This is normally a joint venture (JV). Coalescing is less formal than contracting and is in fact, common in high-tech industries where the obligations cannot be so precisely defined as in contracting.

JVs require a sharing of expertise and resources. And the JVs are usually more successful when the two organisations are of equal power. And that they can offer complementary skills, have similar outlooks on the way to operate in their industry, and each finds that they cannot go into it alone.

Often, JVs are made with direct competitors which reduces competition in the area over which co-operation is occurring, but usually only for a specific duration. The aim of the JV is usually that ultimately the new company should become a self-standing entity with its own staff and strategic aims quite distinct from those of its parent shareholders. An excellent example of a JV is Unilever, set up by a Dutch and an English company in the 1920s, and this JV has grown into a major multinational corporation.

Let us review some of the potential problems of coalescing or JVs. One such problem is that because different groups come together to exchange ideas, their views or operating procedures may be vastly different; this may then create conflict. Conflict may also arise out because of cultural differences, particularly so in JVs comprising companies of different nationalities. Then again, conflicts may also arise with regard to profit distribution.

JVs, in attempting to cut costs and effect efficiency, may also reduce or retrench their now enlarged combined staff. It can be quite unsettling, trying in the initial period, and in a JV, the way the organisation is structured may also create problems for all parties involved. There could be co-ordination problems. And a limit may also exist to the degree to which the company's technical expertise/ knowledge can be transferred and the other to learn or absorb the necessary expertise. Either party may <u>not</u> regard the other party as equal. Indeed, a marriage of unequals is difficult to sustain, and is doomed to fail.

5   Co-opting

Co-opting is absorbing outside elements into an organisation's management, that is, as is seen when outside directors are appointed onto the company's board of directors. Usually leaders from important sector of the company's environment are made part of the company through inter-locking directorships.

Companies operating overseas may at times appoint local directors; they draw upon people with local expertise and knowledge and provide points of contact when problems occur in the operation. The local directors often have strong political or business connections.

Such an arrangement usually tends to be appropriate for an organisation that is relatively weak, vulnerable, or wishes to strengthen itself in a particular segment of the environment.

Some problems may exist with co-opting from the perspective of a focal organisation. Indeed, the co-opted individuals may become more involved in the management of the organisation than was originally intended and autonomy can then be lost. Co-opting indeed puts an obligation on the focal organisation to accept any advice given; hence an organisation tends to lose autonomy through such a device. Besides, decisions are made by only a limited number of individuals in the organisation (i.e. senior management, CEO, etc.). The outside directors' views may also be biased, and thus decisions made may <u>not</u> be in the company's best interests. And the decisions made may also <u>not</u> reflect that of the organisation's goals / objectives.

On the whole, when partnering, a company's partner must be one with the complementary assets, that is, to supply some of the resource or competencies needed to achieve the partnership or alliance objectives.

According to Oliver, C. (1990), these complementary needs may come about in various circumstances:

O **Legal necessity** as required legally, more so in developing countries, where the international company must take a local partner before being granted permission to do business.

O **Asymmetry**. Alliances are usually formed between powerful companies and not-so powerful ones with specifically needed assets such as technical skills. The aim is to increase market share for the more influential company.

O **Reciprocity**. Where the two partners' assets have reciprocal strength(s), synergies exist and that the alliance leads to greater power than the two companies could hope to exercise separately.

O **Efficiency**. Where an alliance leads to lower joint costs in many critical areas such as scale, procurement and others, this serves as a powerful stimulus to alliance formation.

O **Reputation**. Alliances also boost the image, prestige and reputation of the partners. It gives the partners' products and services a higher profile in the market place.

Cultural fit must exist between the partners in the alliance. The relationship between the partners as in a marriage is a key to the success of the arrangement. Appropriate attitudes must prevail between partners, and they are *commitment* and *trust*. Lack of commitment can easily kill an alliance in a short time while trust needs to be developed very early in the relationships.

In a <u>Harvard Business Review</u> article, *Collaborative Advantage: The Art of Alliances*, Kanter, Rosabeth Moss (1994: 100) speaks of the "eight I's that create successful we's", that "effective intercompany relationships" and that "true partnerships that tend to meet certain criteria":

1 "**Individual excellence**. both partners are strong and have something of value to contribute to the relationship. Their motives for entering into the relationships are positive (to pursue future opportunities), not negative (to mask weaknesses or escape a difficult situation).

2 **Importance**. The relationship fits major strategy objectives of the partners, so they want to make it work. Partners have long-term goals in which the relationship plays a key role.

3 **Interdependence**. The partners need each other. They have complementary assets and skills. Neither can accomplish alone what both can together.

4 **Investment**. The partners invest in each other (for example, through equity swaps, cross-ownership, or mutual board service) to demonstrate their respective stakes in the relationship and each other. They show tangible signs of long-term commitment by devoting financial and other resources to the relationship.

5 **Information**. Communication is reasonably open. Partners share information required to make the relationship work, including their objectives and goals, technical data, and knowledge of conflicts, trouble spots, or changing situations.

6 **Integration**. The partners develop linkages and shared ways of operating so they can work together smoothly. They

build broad connections between many people at many organisational levels. Partners become both teachers and learners.

7   **Institutionalisation.** The relationship is given a formal status, with clear responsibilities and decision processes. It extends beyond the particular people who formed it, and it cannot be broken on a whim.

8   **Integrity.** The partners behave toward each other in honorable ways that justify and enhance mutual trust. They do not abuse the information they gain, nor do they undermine each other."

Comparisons and Contrasts between the 2 Types of Strategies

Overall, both strategies are concerned with ensuring the company's survival as well as up-keeping of its profits. In my opinion, any company, engaging in either of these strategies, must be innovative. While certainly, those engaging in competitive strategies must innovate because of increasing competition – their rivals may outdo them, those with co-operative strategies must also continue to update their processes, not just taking comfort in their partners' or network's resources and strengths. In the latter, remaining complacent means their partners can seriously overwhelm or engulf them.

However, in competitive strategies, organisations are fighting for scarce resources while in co-operative strategies, companies are exchanging or sharing resources as well as avoiding resource scarcity. Competitive strategies involve much suspicion, arm's length and short-term contracts while co-operative strategies involve much trust, add value to both sides, high commitment and longer-term contracts. With co-operative strategies, the performance of organisations can be enhanced by inter-organisational relationships because it helps the organisations to get things done efficiently. A synergistic effect can influence both organisations.

Whatever strategies – competitive or co-operative – adopted, the whole logic of it is to ensure the company's long term success. And companies must work towards creating and growing their organisational excellence.

Internal Organisational Traits Contributing to Long-term Company Success

Next, several organisational traits that are associated with excellent companies can be identified. Let us discuss these internal organisational traits.

Corporate leaders and mangers should not only develop strategies for interacting with the outside environment, but also build internal organisational traits that contribute to long-lasting company success. "The smart organization is the one that survives" (Lawrence Lyons).

Top Management

Good management is the key to long-term organisational success. And to achieve its goals efficiently, an organisation principally depends on the calibre of its (top) managers. Successful companies' top management usually has the vision of what the company can be and what it stands for. Top management must also have clear vision and objectives as well as the ability to clarify roles and direction (Mann, R. W., 1990). The top management has a bias for action too. Setting the tone for the company, the top management also promotes a foundation of core values.

Top management teams are crucial to strategic success. Hambrick D. C. (1989) notes that "team qualities are the essential foundation for a successful strategic process within the firm", and highlights "open mindedness", "perseverance", "communication skills", and "vision" as key competency areas. "The business with a top team whose qualities are well suited to emerging trends in the environment, as well forming a complementary whole, will have the best chance of competitive success" Hambrick D. C. (1989).

Strategic Orientation

Weak companies, on one hand, suffer from a misalignment of visions. Different, varying views of the company's overall vision exists and these permeate at every level of the company.

Excellent companies, on the other hand, have a clear business focus and goals. They lead rather than follow. Excellent companies are usually customer-driven, providing fast response to their customers.

Successful companies look at customers ahead. They anticipate customer's needs before even the customers do; they anticipate and create new markets.

According to Nicholas Imparato and Oren Harari in their book Jumping the Curve: Innovation and Strategic Choice in an Age of Transition, successful organisations develop processes that maximise the flow of knowledge and information. Information technology (IT) is used to link internal resources, external resources and customers; there is this building of the company around the software and the software around the customer.

Flexible and Adaptable

Organisations with tall hierarchies and narrow spans of control tend to be bureaucratic and 'mechanistic'. Such organisations are usually rigid and slow in adapting to changes in the environment. Or worse, to paraphrase Charles Handy, the managers of these organisations, having been brought up on a diet of power, divide and rule, have been indeed preoccupied with authority rather than making things happen with the business as effective as it can. And Sam Walton in Sam Walton: Made in America, once said these: "… a lot of bureaucracy is really the product of some empire builder's ego. Some folks have a tendency to build up big staffs around them to emphasise their own importance, and we don't need any of that at Wal-mart. If you're not serving the customer, or supporting the folks who do, we don't need you". Indeed, "many executives feel it is good to have control. They become addicted to power – and that is what kills companies" – Manfred Kets De Vries.

Bureaucratic organisational structures are accused of many sins, including inefficiency, demeaning, and routinised work that alienates both employees and the customers a company wants to serve. Besides, "mechanistic approaches create organizational forms that have difficulty in adapting to change. Like machines, mechanistic organisations are designed to achieve pre-determined goals. They are not designed for innovation" (Gareth Morgan; 1998: 32).

On the other hand, successful companies are usually those that are flexible and adaptable to the chaotic changes of the environment. They are usually better in organisational design. That is, they have simple form with leaner staff, and are essentially decentralised and responsive to changes in the environment and markets.

Or better still, organisations should be like termite colonies, a term used by Gareth Morgan (1998: 326) in his book, Images of Organisation. "Work in the termite colony reflects a self-organising process where order emerges 'out of chaos'. While the nest always has a familiar pattern, it is infinitely variable in terms of detailed form. It is impossible to predict the detailed structure in advance, because it emerges as a result of scattered pattern of droppings. This is what makes the construction process so different than that of human beings. The 'masterpiece' evolves from random, chaotic activities guided by what seems to be an *overall* sense of purpose and direction, but in an open-ended manner." Termites then are "master builders" and thus "provide inspiration for developing coherent approaches to strategic management and change, without the straitjackets and problems imposed by trying to follow predetermined plans" (Gareth Morgan, 1998: 324).

Flatter Organisational Structures

Hierarchies have not disappeared and indeed, they are not likely to ever do so. But they have been reduced with organisations becoming leaner and fitter.

Of great theoretical and practical importance, I would argue that having a flatter and decentralised organisation structure would benefit the company, and contribute to long-lasting company success. The successful organisation is based on participation. The company would have self-managing teams or task forces, created to spearhead the company's new ideas or implement changes. With the presence of such (participative) teams dealing with various issues at any point in time, **decision making are 'pushed down' the line with employees having more opportunity to decide**. Employees are empowered at the company's operational level and they decide their goals with a sense of control over their time. The empowered employees are likely to feel accountable for the job to be done at hand, taking personal responsibility for the success or failure of their job.

With flatter structures too, **the employees or people are given more opportunities to self-actualise themselves**. They are given chances of exposure to higher-level jobs and they develop their potentials as well.

In one of the authors' book <u>Strategic Customer Management: Enhancing Customer retention and Service Recovery</u>, he mentioned that "employees must lead and leaders must work towards service recovery and success!" To elaborate, leadership gives much energy to work and must be felt throughout the organisation. Employees lead to create the atmosphere in providing excellence service to customers and top management work hard to set the right direction, channelling their efforts in making this atmosphere possible. Top management must be willing to grant responsibility, give authority and reward with appropriate incentives to sustain such an atmosphere. There is **massive effect of leadership and pro-activeness**.

W. Edwards once mentioned that "you don't have to please the boss; you have to please the customer" (Ettore, Barbara; 1995: 19 - 23). In an unempowered organisations, constant referrals to the higher management (as if to please the bosses and meet their needs) for decisions take time, leading to the customers' feeling that the organisation is inefficient, and the customer may take his business elsewhere. **Through empowerment, however, the people**

learn and know what tools to use to resolve issues or recover service breakdowns on the spot without referring to higher management. And when people are empowered, they feel more motivated – feeling "charged" in the position to solve problems, making intelligent decisions, and resolving issues.

In a flat-structure organisation with a wide span of control or fewer levels, the employees can also communicate easily with the top management. **The top management gets a better idea of what is happening at the operational level.** Their ears are on the ground! They would then be able to better appreciate the operational concerns; thus, giving more empathetic support or even resources. This would in a way enhance the relationships between the people at the top and their people. Such strong rapport once created would be an asset to the company; the people would feel better appreciated for their efforts and be more willing to stay.

In fact, as the self-directing teams or task forces deal with the project from beginning to end, they know exactly how the task or job begins and how it should end. Indeed **being able to see the big picture, they know how significant their tasks or jobs affect the company as a whole**.

Close rapport between team members and top management also facilitates performance feedback, and this enables employees to correct any mistakes responsively or quickly along the way. After all, they know that their efforts can affect the company's profits or losses.

Indeed, **a flat and decentralised structure can also spur employees' innovation**. Such a structure helps to get rid of the headquarters mentality where everything or every decision comes from the top or centre. Every employee is to have a say or input into the decision making process, and innovative solutions can surely come about. This would certainly lead to a more vibrant workplace for the company's employees. And if we were to transfer or extend this to the national administrative level, a more participative spirit would be said to emerge. Singapore, at the point of writing, is considering the running of the country administration under 5 to

6 divisional districts; each district is to be managed by the mayor of CDC (Community Development Councils) who is then responsible for running the estate as well as building a sense of community.

Good relationships between the top management and employees can be also a boon; the **employees would be more willing to share their ideas with management**. They put in extra efforts, suggesting, contributing and making the whole organisation more entrepreneurial. And once their ideas are accepted, the staff themselves quickly implement them, giving the organisation an edge over the competition.

Self-directing Teams

typically consist of five to thirty workers with different skills who rotate jobs, produce an entire product or service range and who take over managerial duties such as work and vacation scheduling, ordering materials, and hiring new members.

The Self-directing team design usually consists of permanent teams, and has these three features or elements:

1. The team is given **access to resources** such as materials, information, equipment, machinery, supplies, etc. needed to perform a complete task.

2. **The team has and includes a range of employee skills** such as engineering, manufacturing, finance, and marketing. The team eliminates barriers between departments, functions, disciplines, or specialities. Team members are cross-trained to perform each another's job, and the combined skills are sufficient to perform a major organisation task.

3. The team is **empowered with decision-making authority** that means members have the freedom to plan, solve problems, set priorities, spend money, monitor results and co-ordinate activities with other departments or teams. The team has the autonomy to do what is necessary to accomplish its task(s).

Volvo, for example, uses self-directing teams of seven to ten hourly-workers, and each team assembling four cars per shift. Team members are trained to handle all assembly jobs, creating greater employee motivation and lower absenteeism. It was also reported that General Mills too increased the productivity of its plants by 40% when using self-directed teams.

****

Some Key Benefits of Self-directing Teams

Self-directing teams bring several benefits to organisations; these include the fact that the self-directing teams:

1   Enable service improvements, i.e., speedy and efficient delivery of goods and services to the company customers. Quicker decision-making process, with rapid response time, exists in team environment that results in greater customer satisfaction.
2   Eliminate barriers and in fact, practically little barriers exist among the departments, which means co-operation among the various departments with the company's total task(s) or goal(s) in mind.
3   Boost employee morale; the people are enthused about their involvement and participation.
4   Reduce the company's administrative overheads; the teams can take on the various administrative tasks.

****

Innovative and Learning from Mistakes

Winning-edge companies are also innovative companies, learning from their mistakes. Here, the best Asian company example is that of Honda, its "secret to innovation", being "honest and receptive". "It is easy for people to make mistakes" and that "when you make a mistake or something fails, you can learn from taking in other people's views or ideas... ... (yet) honesty and receptivity can be surprisingly difficult especially when one is on the verge of succeeding at a hard-won task. When it fails, accepting the failure and taking in new ideas is the fastest way to advance. Honda's progress bears this out." (The NHK Group, 1996: 52).

Corporate Culture and People Resources

Philip Sadler (1991, 1998: 14) defines the corporate culture as "an amalgam of shared values, a common 'mindset', characteristic behaviours and symbols of various kinds". In other words, corporate culture is 'the way we do things here' or 'what has been generally accepted by us'. Some examples of such values include resilience or toughness, industriousness, pragmatism, profits, customer service and other values.

For companies to have long-term success, companies must get rid of the idea of valuing positions as career goals in favour of portraying a career as a succession of bigger projects and accomplishments. And of new skills learnt.

Positions are out. The concept of position is part of the outdated static concept of the organisation. Projects and processes are in! Management or authority is out; leadership and personal power is in!

People are critical and emphasising the human capital value is vital to a company's long- term success. T. J. Watson Jr. (the son of the founder of International Business Machines (IBM) used the metaphor of "wild ducks" to illustrate the kind of employees needed by IBM. He said, "You can make wild ducks tame, but you can never make tame ducks wild again", meaning freedom and opportunity ("wild ducks") must be made available to keep from taming creative employees at IBM.

And Honda founder, Soichiro Honda deliberately hired other mavericks who were typically college dropouts or rejects from traditional, more established companies (Pearson and Ehrlich, 1990). Indeed, companies benefit from recruiting and retaining creative and innovative employees.

While weak companies usually give lip service to the importance of people as assets, excellent companies are better able to tap their people resources, their energies and enthusiasm. They do this by creating a trusting climate, encouraging productivity through people and taking a long-term view. "Putting people before products" (Matsushita), the company people can then work and deal openly with one another. Collaboration across departments and divisions need trust. The people can also work together, helping to resolve problems. Productivity through people basically means the active involvement and participation of the rank-and-file people. The people are empowered, and after all, they are considered as the root of quality and productivity. Winning companies also take a long view of things, regarding their people as "diamonds in the rough" (Matsushita). These companies train their investment, staying committed to their people as assets for the long term.

Corporate culture, according to Philip Sadler (1991, 1998: 82 - 83), can have tremendous effect on the company people. They can "'be turned' on and become committed:

O   when the values are clearly articulated and they are constantly reinforced.
O   the values are the ones they can identify with and adopt as their own.
O   top management 'lives' the values."

Your Notes, Ideas
& Action Points

Chapter 8

Epilogue

"To accomplish great things we must not only act but also dream,
not only plan but also believe."
Anatole France

"The major challenge for leaders in the twenty-first century will be how to release the brainpower of their organisations."
Warren Bennis

All of us have to shed our old patterns or methods of thinking. A snake has to shed its old skin to allow growth and change to happen. We need to think on our feet, think strategically and develop new paradigms or mental models to grow our organisation.

Be forward-looking. Planning and strategic thinking has their benefits. Your investing time and effort in doing preparation and strategic thinking will enhance your self-confidence as well as developing powerful ways to boost your marketability. Be rewarded; use our imagination. Think, stretch and extend ourselves, enabling us to get ahead in our careers.

Strategy is often taught as if it were basically conceptual in nature, concerned mainly with ideas of the business future and reducing uncertainties. To be effective, strategy must take effect in behaviour (how everyone in the company sets goals and every day, thinks and acts) and should be action-based as well as ongoing. The plan for action must be followed up and monitored to ensure goal attainments.

The authors would like to end the book with our little poem and two stories that have become our personal favourites.

For the poem, here it is:

> Build yourself through planning
> Grow your potential by goal-setting.
> You're not that tiny,
> Be a master of your destiny
> Think of possibilities,
> Optimise your abilities.
> Prevention rather than cure,
> making your success endure
> Forward thinking
> Lateral thinking
> Thinking on our feet,
> Your rivals will quit!
> Recreate… a new you born
> Move on, on and on…
> While the sun shines, make hay
> every day, day by day.

And we find these two age-old wisdom stories found in the Aesop's fables, still very relevant in our present day context. And here they go.

Story number one (#1) is about the frogs and the well. Two frogs lived together in the marsh. However, one hot summer, the marsh dried up. They the left looking for a better place to live in, for frogs like damp places if they can get them. By and by, they came to a deep well, and one of them said to the other, "This is good, looks like a very nice cool place. Let's jump and make home out of it!" But the other, the wiser one replied, "Not so fast, my friend. Supposing this well dried up like the marsh, how should we get out again?"

As you would have guessed, the moral of the story is, of course: Think twice before you act. Look before you leap.

The second story (#2) is about the mouse and the bull. A bull gave chase to the mouse that had bitten him in the nose. But the Mouse was too quick for him, slipped into the hole in the wall; and the bull charged furiously into the wall again and again. Tired, he then sank down on the ground completely exhausted. When all was quiet again, the mouse darted out and bit the bull again. The bull then started in its feet bellowing with rage, and the mouse was then back to its hole again. The bull could do nothing but bellow and fume! And he heard a shrill tiny voice say from inside the wall, "You big fellows don't always have it your own way. Sometimes, you see, the little ones come off best." How very true! God's not always on the side of big battalions. The battle is not always to the strong!

We need to think. It is when we stop thinking or rflecting that we often miss opportunities.

Remember "Just do it", Nike's slogan? Now, let's do it.

The things that I need to do (please indicate the **deadline/ dates**) after reading this book, that is, my follow-up action steps. I must ensure that they become my action steps, <u>not</u> stops! I'm committed to remembering these:

> *"In order to be saved you must know what you believe,*
> *know why you believe it,*
> *and know how to act upon it."*
> St Thomas Aquinas

> *"Things won are done; joy's soul lies in the doing."*
> William Shakespeare

1 _____
2 _____
3 _____
4 _____
5 _____
6 _____

7 _____

8 _____

9 _____

10 _____

11 _____

12 _____

Useful References

Barnard, Chester (1938). *The Functions of the Executive*, Cambridge, Mass. Harvard University, p. 19.

Cleary, T. (1991). *The art of war – Sun Tzu* (translated). Shambala, China.

Daft, Richard (1998) (6th edition) *Organization Theory and Design*, U.S.A., SOUTH-WESTERN College Publishing.

Dreher, D. (1996). *The Tao of personal leadership*, HarpersCollins Publishers: United States.

Drucker, Peter F. (1954). *The Practice of Management*, New York, Harper and Row, p. 62 - 87

Ettore, Barbara (1995) *Retooling People and Processes*, *Management Review* (June 1995), p. 19 - 23.

Gagliardi, G. (2011). 'Sun Tzu in competition with chivalry', 21 September 2011. ChivalryToday.com Website: http://chivalrytoday.com/competing-chivalry-sun-tzu/ Accessed on 27 November 2014.

Healthfield, S.M. (2014). 'Change Management Wisdom', humanresources.about.com. Website: http://humanresources.about.com/od/changemanagement/a/change_wisdom.htm?utm_term=wisdom%20and%20strategy&utm_content=p1-main-1-title&utm_medium=sem-sub&utm_source=msn&utm_campaign=adid-b3b06591-dfe5-4a6f-a88a-7b0c04c0788c-0-ab_msb_ocode-28815&ad=semD&an=msn_s&am=broad&q=wisdom%20and%20strategy&dqi=&o=28815&l=sem&qsrc=1&askid=b3b06591-dfe5-4a6f-a88a-7b0c04c0788c-0-ab_msb Accessed on 25 November 2014.

Horsager, D. (2012). 'You can't be a great leader without trust. Here's how you Build It', 24 Oct 2012, Forbes. Website: http://www. forbes.com/sites/forbesleadershipforum/2012/10/24/you-cant-be-a-great-leader-without-trust-heres-how-you-build-it/ Accessed on 25 November 2014.

Imparato, Nicholas and Harari, Oren (1994) *Jumping the Curve: Innovation and Strategic Choice in an Age of Transition*, Jossey-Bass.

Kanter Rosabeth Moss (1994) *Collaborative Advantage: The Art of Alliances* in <u>Harvard Business Review</u> July – August 1994, Harvard Business School, p. 96 - 108.

Krause, D.G. (1997). *The way of the leader*, Nicholas Brealey: Great Britain.

Lassere, Philippe and Schutte, Hellmut (1995) *Strategies for Asia Pacific*, Macmillan Business: Great Britain.

Leeson, N. (1997). *Rogue trader: Nick Leeson – His own amazing story*, Time Warner, U.K.

Low, K. C. P. (2014). 'Key leadership insights and lessons from ancient wisdom', *International journal of business and social science*, Vol. 5 No. 4 [Special Issue – March 2014], p. 172-180.

Low, K.C.P. (2013). 'Are you MAD enough? If not, how would you have grown your career?', *Educational Research*, (ISSN: 2141-5161) Vol. 4(6), June 2013, p. 497-505.

Low, K. C. P. (2013a). *Leading successfully in Asia*, Springer: Heidelberg, Germany/ U.K./ USA.

Low, K. C. P. (2010). 'Applying strategic leadership, the way of the Dragon', *e-Leader Chinese American Scholars' Association (CASA) Conference*, 4 - 6 January 2010, Singapore.

Low, K. C. P. (2010a). *Successfully negotiating in Asia*, Springer: Heidelberg, Germany.

Low, K. C. P. (2009). 'The way of the dragon: Some strategic leadership Ways', *Leadership & organizational management journal*, Volume 2009 Issue 2, p. 40 - 59.

Low, K. C. P. (2009a). 'Strategic maintenance & leadership excellence in Place marketing – The Singapore perspective', *Business journal for entrepreneurs*, Volume 2009, Issue 3, p. 125 - 143.

Low, K. C. P. (2008). 'How to win big in place marketing battlefield – Formula One night race, the Singapore perspective', *Business journal for entrepreneurs*, Volume 2008 Issue 4, p. 115 - 125.

Low, K. C. P. (2006). 'Fraud prevention/ Management and corporate values – The Singapore perspective', *Business journal for entrepreneurs*, p. 56 - 75.

Low, K.C.P. (2000). *Opportunities and Survival Strategies, Horizons*, Magazine of the Management Development Institute of Singapore (MDIS), Singapore, MDIS, Jan/Feb 2000, p. 10 - 12.

Low, K. C. P. and Teo T. C. J. (2014) Some Chinese War Strategies – Applying Its Key Lessons to Strategic Leadership', *International Journal of Business and Social Science*, vol. 5, no. 12; Nov 2014, p. 91 – 99.

MSG: Management Study Guide (2013). 'Strategic leadership – Definition and qualities of a strategic leader', Management Study Guide. Website: http://managementstudyguide.com/strategic-leadership.htm Accessed on 26 November 2014.

Mann, R. W. (1990) *A Building Blocks Approach to Strategic Change* in *Training and Development Journal*, August 1990, p. 23 - 25.

Maxwell, J. C. (1993). *Developing the leader within you*, Thomas Nelson, Inc.: USA.

McMillan, Ian and McGrath, R. G. (1997) *Discovering Points of Differentiation* in *Harvard Business Review*, July - August 1997, p. 3 - 11.

McCann, Dick and Stewart, Jan (1997) *Aesop's Management Fables*, Oxford, Butterworth-Hienemann.

McCormack Mark. H. (1995, 1996) *On Managing*, Great Britain, Arrow Business Books.

Michaelson, G.A. (2001). *Sun Tzu, the art of war for managers*, Adams Media Corporation: Canada.

Michaelson, G. A. and Michaelson, S.W. (2010). *Sun Tzu: The Art of War for Managers: 50 Strategic Rules Updated for Today's Business*, Adams Media Corporation: Holbrook, MA.

Morgan, Gareth (1998) *Images of Organization* (The Executive Edition), U.S.A., Berrett-Koehler Publishers & Sage Publications, Inc.

Niven, D. (2000). *The 100 simple secrets of happy people*, HarperCollins Publishers: New York.

Oliver, C (1990) *Determinants of Interorganisational Relationships: Integration and Future Directions*, AMR, Vol. 15, No. 2.

Owen, J. (2012). *The leadership skills handbook*, Kogan Page Ltd.: Great Britain.

PHP/ Matsushita Konosuke (1994) *Matsushita Konosuke (1894 - 1989) His Life and Legacy*, Japan, PHP Institute, Inc.

Pearson, A. E. and Ehrlich, S. P. (1990) *Honda Motor Company and Honda of America*, Case No. 9-390-111, Harvard Business School.

Pfeffer,. J. and Salancik, G. (1978). *The External Control of Organisations*, New York Harper.

Price, James L. (1972) *The Study of Organizational Effectiveness*, Sociological Quarterly 13, 3 - 15.

Pencak, S. (2014). 'Strategy quotes', Magnetic Look. Website: http://www.mymagneticblog.com/strategy-quotes/ Accessed on 27 November 2014.

Porter, Michael (1996) *What is Strategy? Harvard Business Review*, Nov - Dec 1996, USA, Harvard Business School.

Quick, J. C. and Nelson, D. L. (2013) (8th ed.) *Principles of Organizational Behavior: Realities and Challenges*, South-Western Cengage Learning: China.

Ries, Al and Trout, Jack (1997) *Focused in a Fuzzy World* in Rethinking the Future, UK., Biddles Ltd., p. 185.

Sadler, Philip (1991, 1998). 3rd edition, *Designing Organizations*, Institute of Directors/ Kogan Page, Great Britain.

The NHK Group (1996). *Good Mileage – The High Performance Business Philosophy of Soichiro Honda*, Singapore, NHK Publishing, p. 52.

Woopidoo! (2014). 'Strategy quotes', Woopidoo.com Website: http://www.woopidoo.com/business_quotes/strategies-quotes.htm Accessed on 26 November 2014.

The Authors

Teck Choon **TEO**

Education

Doctor of Business Administration (DBA) University of South Australia 2003
Master of Education (M.Ed)(Leadership, Policy & Change) Monash University 2004
Master of Management (M.M.) Macquarie University 2002
Master of Arts (M.A.) Macquarie University 1997

Biography

Currently, Dr. Teo is the Head of Department at London School of Business and Finance (LSBF) Singapore, having been in the private educational institutions sector for the past 14 years. He is an Adjunct Professor at Concordia University of Chicago and regularly teaches Managing Human Capital and Organisational Behaviour courses. He is an active board member of the Chinese American Scholar

Association (CASA) based in New York since 2015 and has written several research papers ranging from management, human resource, leadership and more recently learning styles, cultural influence and learning strategies.

Selected Publications

- Teo, T.C. (2015), Tsunami Leadership, Organisational Turmoil and Mayhem, E-Leader International Journal, Vol. 10, Number 2, http://www.g-casa.com ISSN 1935-4819, Chinese American Scholars Association, New York, New York, USA, Jul
- Teo, T.C., Zhang, A.C. and Low, K.C.P. (2015), Corruption in South Sudan: A Business Perspective, Singapore Management Journal, Vol. 4, No. 1, December 2015
- Teo, T.C. and Low, K.C.P. (2016), Facilitating Adult Learning in Private Educational Institutions in Singapore: A Singaporean Perspective, E-Leader International Journal, Vol. 11, Number 2, http://www.g-casa.com ISSN 1935-4819, Chinese American Scholars Association, New York, New York, USA, Jul
- Loh, C.Y. and Teo, T.C. (2016), Students' Perception of Collaborative Learning, Conflict Management and Satisfaction in a Private Educational Institution Learning Environment: An Asian Case Study, Journal of Education & Social Policy, Vol. 3, No. 3 August 2016
- Loh, C.Y. and Teo, T.C. (2016), Understanding Asian Students Learning Styles, Cultural Influence and Learning Strategies, Journal of Education & Social Policy, Vol. 7, No. 1 March 2017

He can be contacted at johnttc@singnet.com.sg

Request/ Enquiries

We have a request! Do share your success stories with us! And if you have any comments about the book, we are always interested in your feedback. We are eager to hear from you, please write to us.

Kim Cheng Patrick **LOW**

Effective 26 May 2017, Prof. Dr. Patrick Low is appointed as Director, Scientific (Research) Center and Dean of Construction Technologies, Infrastructure and Management of Kazakh American University/ Kazakh Leading Academy of Architecture and Civil Engineering (KazGASA) for 8-month period until 2 Jan 2018 (The Republic of Kazakhstan's Ministry of Education & Science-sponsored).

Currently, Prof. Dr. Patrick Low is a Visiting Professor with the University of the South Pacific's (Suva, Fiji) *Master of Business Administration - Human Resource Management program.* He has decades of experience which includes managing, consulting, training in various companies and universities plus running his own HRD enterprise. Patrick has passionately imparted his in-depth industrial experience and conceptual knowledge of human resources, negotiation, leadership, marketing, performance management and personal effectiveness. He attained an *International PhD in Business and Management, University of South Australia* and a *Master of Business, CURTIN University of Technology.* His many professional qualifications include the *Chartered Marketer (CIM, UK); Chartered Consultant* and an *Accredited Professional Consultant (American Consultants' League).* He has authored several books and (co)authored many book chapters and publications.

Since the late '80s, Patrick has been a HR professional and was the *Senior Training Manager, Management Development (Asia Pacific Region), Standard Chartered Bank* and the *UOB Bank.* He has worked in the Civil Service, electronics, trade and financial industries. He has conducted exclusive fraud management courses for banks and companies. He has completed HRD projects in all ASEAN countries, HK, Bangladesh and Sri Lanka.

From 1995 - April 2014, he managed his own firm - *BusinesscrAFT™ Consultancy* and completed consultancy projects for many organisations including: *Comserv, Hornbill Airways, Islamic Bank of Brunei, Eagle's Wings, KAFCO (Bangladesh), Khind Marketing, KKB Engineering Sdn. Bhd, Kotobuki, Matsushita Electric Singapore, Maybank, MINDEF, Maersk Singapore, MIS (Sales Academy), NTUC, Nam Ho Travel, Natsteel, National Healthcare Group, Rimbunan Hijau, Sarawak Forestry Corporation, Sarawak State Library, Singapore National Employers' Federation, Singapore National Co-operative Federation, SESCO, Sarawak Craft Council, Standard Chartered Bank, Tan Tock Seng Hospital, Trans-Link Express.*

Prof Low has been a faculty member of several universities:

- 2007–2013: Taught Masters Management and Organizational Behaviour and several undergraduate Organizational studies subjects in the *Universiti Brunei Darussalam (UBD)*
- 2009: *UBD's Deputy Dean of Postgraduate and Research* and an *Associate of the University of South Australia.*
- 2007 Jan–Feb: *Visiting Professor of University of Malaya*
- 2004-2006: *Associate Dean and Professor of Management and Marketing at the Kazakhstan Institute of Management, Economics and Strategic Research (KIMEP).* He was appointed as *Acting Dean* in 2006 Summer.
- Taught HR Management, Organisational Behaviour, Marketing and International Business for *Universities of London, Bradford (U.K.); Murdoch; Monash (Australia)* and *Ngee Ann Polytechnic.*

Qualifications

- PhD in Business and Management, University of South Australia
- Master of Business, CURTIN University of Technology
- Bachelor of Arts (Singapore)
- Chartered Marketer (CIM, UK)
- Chartered Consultant and an Accredited Professional Consultant (American Consultants' League)
- Graduate Diploma in Marketing (UK)
- Graduate Diploma in Personnel Management (SIM / SIPM)
- Graduate Diploma in the Marketing of Financial Services (MIS)
- Certificate in Administrative Management / Organisation & Methods.
- Licensed administrator, user and interpreter of **MBTI** and **DISC**-certified profiling instruments.

Achievements

- 2017 (1 May): Ranked as one of the top 30,000 authors in the Social Science Research Network: SSRN
- 2017 (23 Oct): Ranked as one of the top 10,000 authors in the Social Science Research Network: SSRN
- 2014: He was awarded *Research Excellence* 2013 by *Franklin Publications* (USA).
- 2004/5: *Researcher of the Year 2004/5* for *Bang College of Business, Kazakhstan Institute of Management, Economics and Strategic Research (KIMEP)*.
- 1994: He was awarded the *MIS / Standard Chartered Gold Medal Award* for being the most outstanding graduate in the Graduate Diploma in Marketing of Financial Services.

Prof Low is the author of several books including"

- *Team Success* (2013)
- *Leading Successfully in Asia* (2013) (now moving into its 2nd edition)
- *Successful Negotiating in Asia.* (2010)
- *Strategic Customer Management* - 2006 (3rd.edition), 2002 revised, 2000. As featured in *Asian Entrepreneur* 2003, this is one of Border's Top 10 Business Books.
- *Sales Success* (2005; 2006) (now moving into its 3rd edition)

He was an advisory board member of the *Emerald Insight's Management Decision* (2007 – 2014), Prof Low was also the Section Editor of Springer's *Dictionary of Corporate Social Responsibility* (2015), *Encyclopedia of Corporate Social Responsibility* (2014) and was the Chief Editor for *Corporate Social Responsibility in Asia* (2014). He also managed several co-authors in writing several Corporate Social Responsibility topics in these two books.

He can be contacted at patrick_low2003@yahoo.com

Index

"For the several last years, I was searching for some useful tips in a real-life book that will teach us on how to act strategically especially in different situations.

So when I read parts of the book I feel that this is the book that I was searching for. I learnt how to plan and how to properly use our potentials to be the leader of our own life.

It is the must-read book for everyone from marketing specialists to the economists or in fact, any professionals."

Yermek Abilgaziyev, MA in Politics and Security in Central Asia from the Organization for Security and Co-operation in Europe (OSCE) Academy. Senior Specialist at the KazGASA University.

"A SURE WINNER… filled with valuable tips and pointers!"

Dr. Elmira Ibrayeva
Doctor of Sciences (International Relations), MA (Economics)
Associate Professor of Kazakh American University